Journal
of the
Shenandoah Valley
During the
Civil War Era

Volume I
2018

Jonathan A. Noyalas
Editor

A publication of Shenandoah University's McCormick Civil War Institute

Manuscript Submissions and Books for Review

The *Journal of the Shenandoah Valley During the Civil War* is published annually by Shenandoah University's McCormick Civil War Institute. Manuscript submissions can be sent to the editor at **jnoyalas01@su.edu**. Manuscripts should not exceed 10,000 words in length (including footnotes). Books for review consideration can be sent to the editor at the *Journal of the Shenandoah Valley During the Civil War's* editorial home: Jonathan A. Noyalas, director McCormick Civil War Institute, Davis Hall 115, 1460 University Drive, Winchester, VA 22601.

Cover image, detail of Union troops entering Front Royal, courtesy of Jonathan A. Noyalas private collection

Contents

From the Editor

Feature Essays

Artifacts & Personalities

From the Editor

The "*Raison D'être*"

Jonathan A. Noyalas

In the inaugural issue of *Civil War History* published in March 1955 editor Clyde C. Walton, Jr. felt compelled to "explain" the "*Raison D'être*" for a new journal at a time when "more than 600" were "now published in America."[1] Although the number of published journals is exponentially larger more than six decades later, including two academic journals in the field of Civil War era history (*Civil War History* and *The Journal of the Civil War Era*), Shenandoah University's McCormick Civil War Institute believes there is the need for a new annual journal devoted specifically to the study of the Shenandoah Valley during the Civil War era.[2]

Throughout four years of conflict the Shenandoah Valley and its demographically diverse population experienced 326 different military actions and numerous occupations by armies of Blue and Gray.[3] Additionally, during General Robert H. Milroy's occupation of the lower Shenandoah Valley in the first half of 1863, the region became an important proving ground for the active enforcement of President Abraham Lincoln's Emancipation Proclamation. Aside from four years of conflict in the strategically vital region, the Shenandoah Valley holds important connections to

---

[1] Clyde C. Walton, Jr., "An Introduction," *Civil War History* 1 (March 1955): 5.
[2] Since its inception in 2011 *The Journal of the Civil War Era* has only published one essay related to the era in the Shenandoah Valley, Kathryn S. Meier, "'No Place for the Sick': Nature's War on Civil War Soldier and Mental Health in the 1862 Peninsula and Shenandoah Valley Campaigns," *The Journal of the Civil War Era* 1 (June 2011): 176-206. Over the past decade *Civil War History* has published only one essay related to the Shenandoah Valley, Jonathan A. Noyalas, "'The Broader and Purer Purpose': Lessons from the Shenandoah Valley's Monuments and Battlefield Landscapes on Introducing Elements of Civil War Memory to General Audiences," *Civil War History* 62 (June 2016): 186-200.
[3] Shenandoah Valley Battlefields Foundation, *Shenandoah Valley Battlefields National Historic District: Final Management Plan* (New Market, VA: Shenandoah Valley Battlefields Foundation, 2000), i.

personalities and events in the years preceding the secession crisis. In the Civil War's aftermath, the region became the scene of numerous annual gatherings of Union and Confederate veterans; events that at times advanced some degree of healing among former foes, but also reminded veterans of Blue and Gray that the war's bitterness could never be fully expunged.

Although the Shenandoah Valley's Civil War era history is significant, only a small cadre of historians have given it the attention it deserves. The *Journal of the Shenandoah Valley during the Civil War Era* aims to encourage research into and scholarship concerning the era's complexities in the region and to provide a publication outlet in what is Shenandoah University's first academic, peer-reviewed journal.

From examinations of the experiences of African Americans during and after the conflict, the re-evaluation of historic documents, the analysis of historic artifacts, research into personalities who proved important elements of the Shenandoah Valley's Civil War era saga, and to reviews of books related to the region's Civil War era history, this inaugural issue illustrates that there is still much research and scholarship to be done on a region that author Julia Davis characterized as "a legend."[4]

The *Journal's* staff and its editorial board hope that all who read this journal will enjoy it, and historians—whether established or aspiring undergraduates—will be inspired to delve into the complexities and nuances of the Shenandoah Valley's Civil War era history.

---

[4] Julia Davis, *The Shenandoah* (New York: Rinehart & Company, 1945), 2.

"The Time has Come Near that We Will All Have to Learn to Work"
Elite Farm Women of the Lower Shenandoah Valley and Their Slaves During the Civil War

Kenneth E. Koons

Daniel Snyder, a farmer of Clarke County, Virginia, writing to his wife Rachel from a Confederate military encampment in late February of 1863, advised her that "if you find that the negroes will not aid you in your efforts to farm, by studious application to work, you had better sell what corn and provender you have." Apparently, Snyder subsequently received a favorable report from his wife regarding their willingness to work, for in a mid-March letter to her, he expressed his gladness that "Henry and John are so true to you." By late March, however, circumstances had changed dramatically. Snyder wrote that he had been "provoked indeed" by his wife's account of the manner in which Henry and John had spoken to her, and he expressed fear that if such behavior were allowed to continue, they would be "emboldened to do worse." He asserted that "I would rather you should let the land lie idle" and "drive every negro off the place" rather than submit to such behavior.[5] In the lower Shenandoah Valley during the spring of 1863, the Snyders' situation—Daniel away serving in the

---

[5]Daniel C. Snyder, Camp of 11th Reg't Va. Cav., near Edinburg, VA, to Rachel (Louthan) Snyder, Berryville, VA, undated but content suggests late February, 1863; Daniel to Rachel Snyder, March 13, 1863; and Daniel near Harrisonburg, VA, March 29, 1863, to Rachel Snyder, in Daniel C. Snyder Letters, Clarke County Hitorical Association, Berryville, VA. Snyder refers to Henry and John as "negroes." In this instance, Snyder's phrasing in his letter of March 29, 1863, suggests that Henry was hired a slave, and that John was probably a free black working for wages. On slave hiring see John J. Zaborney, *Slaves for Hire: Renting Enslaved Laborers in Antebellum Virginia* (Baton Rouge: Louisiana State University Press, 2012). Discussion of the roles of free blacks in the rural economy of the antebellum Shenandoah Valley may be found in Kenneth E. Koons, "'The Colored Laborers Work as Well as When Slaves': African Americans in the Breadbasket of the Confederacy, 1850-1880" in *Archaeological Perspectives on the American Civil War,* ed. Clarence R. Geier and Stephen R. Potter (Knoxville: University of Tennessee Press, 2000), 233, 237-240.

Confederate army and Rachel trying to manage their farm and supervise the work of an increasingly unreliable work force—became common as bondsmen and women grew ever more restive in the face of the opportunities for freedom that emerged in the chaos of war and federal occupation.

The Civil War thrust Rachel Snyder and other women of Clarke County's farm households into unfamiliar and difficult circumstances. With husbands, fathers, or sons away serving in Confederate armies, the management of farms fell to them. This entailed responsibility for which they were ill-prepared. Moreover, women carried out these roles in harrowing conditions of war and enemy occupation. Often, for example, it was they who dealt with federal soldiers in their dooryards seeking information, horses, forage, or meals. This article provides a case study of how farm women of the lower Shenandoah Valley of Virginia experienced the dissolution of slavery. For evidence, it relies heavily upon a small and geographically concentrated collection of diaries and letters produced by well-to-do and elite farm women of Clarke County as they experienced directly the weakening and collapse of slavery on their farms and in their rural neighborhoods.[6]

In Clarke County, as throughout much of the South during the war, a chief preoccupation of white women of rural slave-owning households was directing and overseeing the work of slaves.[7] In women's accounts of the comings and goings of slaves and descriptions of their interactions with them, we can discern their attitudes about both slaves as people and slavery as an

---

[6] Throughout, I use the term "farm" rather than "plantation" to describe the economic units women presided over and managed in the absence of their husbands, and I refer to "farm women" rather than "planter women." The peculiarities of Clarke County's socio-economic development is such that economic units originating as tobacco-producing "plantations" in the eighteenth century came, by the 1790s, to be called "farms," in consequence of their owners having shifted to the production of wheat. A detailed discussion of these circumstances may be found in Warren R. Hofstra, *A Separate Place: The Formation of Clarke County, Virginia* (White Post, VA: Clarke County Sesquicentennial Committee, 1986; reprint, Madison, WI: Madison House, 1999), 25, 27. Hofstra writes that by the 1790s, "everybody farmed; everybody grew wheat. Frederick County [the parent-county of Clarke] soon became the leading producer of wheat and flour in Virginia. As it did, the term 'planter' dropped out of common usage." This was despite the prevalence in the eastern section of Frederick County (which in 1836 became Clarke County), of wheat growers "with thousands of acres" who "owned scores of slaves" and "produced large quantities of wheat with a semblance of a plantation organization."

[7] Drew Gilpin Faust, *Mothers of Invention: Women of the Slaveholding South in the American Civil War* (Chapel Hill: The University of North Carolina Press, 1996), 53.

institution, and also the circumstances by which slaves fled or were removed from farms during the war. More broadly, the writings of white women illuminate how they and the slaves they owned experienced their relationships with one another during a tumultuous period when both sets of lives were being dramatically transformed by forces beyond their control.[8] Also revealed are the strategies farm women employed to live in a world devoid—or soon to be devoid—of slaves.

Historians who have examined how the Civil War changed women's lives divide generally into two camps—those who argue that women readily exploited new opportunities for independence created by the absence of both husbands and slaves, and those who hold that traditional gender norms, reinforced by a life-long dependence upon slaves, left Southern women utterly unprepared for adjusting to new circumstances, in consequence of which they recoiled from such possibilities.[9] In Clarke County, the absence of slaves caused white women to reshape their lives in a mix of ways more varied and nuanced than either of the polar opposites of this interpretive framework would suggest. Some of them embraced work of the household and farm as their new lot in life, but they did so with an eye to maintaining aspects of the genteel lifestyle that formerly had been enabled by slave labor.

The historical socio-economic development of Clarke County, situated in the lower section of Virginia's Shenandoah Valley, differed singularly from that of the larger region.[10] By 1850,

---

[8] Of course, understanding of the nature of these relationships from the perspective of slaves can be gained only indirectly, through inference based on their behavior and utterances as reported by their owners.

[9] LeeAnn Whites and Alicia P. Long, eds., *Occupied Women: Gender, Military Occupation, and the American Civil War* (Baton Rouge: Louisiana State University Press, 2009), 2. Whites and Long identify Drew Gilpin Faust as a leading proponent of the latter perspective. For her exposition of this view, see *Mothers of Invention*, 7, 78, and passim. Other works that examine encounters between Southern women and Union soldiers and document circumstances regarding the loss of slaves, include Stephen V. Ash, *When the Yankees Came: Conflict and Chaos in the Occupied South, 1861-1865* (Chapel Hill: University of North Carolina Press, 1995); Jacqueline Glass Campbell, *When Sherman Marched North from the Sea: Resistance on the Confederate Home Front* (Chapel Hill: University of North Carolina Press, 2003); Laura F. Edwards, *Scarlett Doesn't Live Here Anymore: Southern Women in the Civil War Era* (Urbana: University of Illinois Press, 2004); and Lisa Tendrich Frank, *The Civilian War: Confederate Women and Union Soldiers during Sherman's March to the Sea* (Baton Rouge: Louisiana State University Press, 2015).

[10] See Hofstra, *A Separate Place*, for a thorough analysis of the early socio-economic and cultural development of Clarke County.

slaves composed nearly 50 percent of the population of the county, whereas in the Shenandoah Valley as a whole the corresponding figure stood at about 20 percent.[11] Also at mid-century, Clarke County farmers produced wheat at levels more than double that of farmers of all other counties of the Valley.[12] A decade later, when war came to the lower Shenandoah Valley, Clarke County farms were subject, perhaps to an unusual degree, to the depredations of federal troops. Farms were large and well-stocked, and included spacious, architecturally stylish homes as well as barns and a host of outbuildings for the processing or storage of foodstuffs. Prosperous looking farms such as these attracted the attention of federal commissary officers, but the high command of their armies also sought to control Clarke County because it lay within a strategically vital stretch of borderland that geographically linked the lower Shenandoah Valley to the nation's capital. In consequence of Clarke's locational importance and its highly productive farms, during much of the war the county was awash with federal troops.[13]

Not surprisingly, farm women's diaries of the period include many bitter complaints about Union soldiers trampling wheat fields, taking livestock, and annoying local inhabitants in a host of other ways. Typical of many diary entries is Sigismunda Stribling Kimball's of mid-March 1862 when she wrote that "three Yankee soldiers came here ... walked across the wheat field, broke open the springhouse door, took out a crock of butter, killed several

---

[11] Koons, "'The Colored Laborers,'" 233.

[12] Figures calculated on the basis of data found in U.S. Census Office, *Statistical View of the United States, ... Being a Compendium of the Seventh Census* (Washington, D.C.: A.O.P. Nicholson, Public Printer, 1854), show that in 1850, farmers through most parts of the Valley produced almost 20 bushels of wheat per capita, while farmers of Clarke County produced almost 42 bushels of wheat per capita. A full discussion of commercial wheat farming as a component of general mixed agriculture, as it was practiced in the nineteenth-century Shenandoah Valley, may be found in Kenneth E. Koons, "'The Staple of Our Country': Wheat in the Regional Farm Economy of the Nineteenth-Century Valley of Virginia," in *After the Backcountry: Rural Life in the Great Valley of Virginia, 1800-1900*, ed. Kenneth E. Koons and Warren R. Hofstra (Knoxville: University of Tennessee Press, 2000), 3-20. Also see Kenneth W. Keller, "The Wheat Trade on the Upper Potomac, 1800-1860," in *After the Backcountry*, 21-33.

[13] Edward H. Phillips, "The Lower Shenandoah Valley during the Civil War: The Impact of War upon the Civilian Population and upon Civil Institutions," (Ph.D. diss., University of North Carolina, 1959), provides thorough description of the damage inflicted by troops (of both sides) as they occupied or moved through rural districts of the lower Shenandoah Valley.

chickens, wrung their necks off and walked away."[14] A week or so later she wrote that at a neighboring farm "the Yankees ... shot all the hogs but ten, seven turkeys, and carried off with them a three year old colt."[15] Kimball encountered federal troops so frequently that month that the rare day when she did not, warranted mention in her diary: "Have not seen a Yankee today—the wonderful thing is now not to see a Yankee." [16] But the Yankee presence continued. In mid-June, Stribling wrote that "Yankees [are] stealing all the horses" and are "about the neighborhood behaving shamefully"— saying that, with no rations, "their orders were to live on the people."[17]

The near-constant presence of Union troops gave farm women much to complain about, but a particular source of concern and even distress among them was the growing realization that control of their slaves had become tenuous. Each of the women whose writings are drawn upon here controlled the labor of a sizeable contingent of slaves. None noted the size of their slave labor forces, but the number of slaves owned by them—or their husbands or other male relatives—in 1860 may be found in slaves' schedules of the federal censuses. Lucy Allen, for example, owned 9 slaves but her brother Edgar, in whose household she lived, owned 37. Mattella Harrison's husband owned 25 slaves. Sigismunda Stribling Kimball and her husband lived in a household headed by her father, who owned 33 slaves. During the war years she controlled the labor of no fewer than 17 slaves. John Louthan, whose numerous daughters kept up a lively correspondence with siblings and other relatives during the war, owned 17 slaves.[18]

Slaves from Clarke County farms were fleeing to freedom as early as the spring of 1862. In May of that year, for example, Kimball

---

[14] Sigismunda Stribling Kimball, Diary, October 14, 1861 to August 29, 1863, Clarke County Historical Association, Berryville, VA, entry for March 12, 1862. This diary has been transcribed by Mary Morris, archivist, Clarke County Historical Association, and I am indebted to her for sharing her transcription with me. This and all subsequent references to the diary are to that transcription.

[15] Ibid., March 23, 1862.

[16] Ibid., March 25, 1862.

[17] Ibid., June 15-16, 1862.

[18] Bureau of the Census, Eighth Census of the United States, 1860, Manuscript Population Schedules, Clarke County, Virginia (Washington, D.C.: National Archives Microfilm Publications, M4322).

noted that a slave from a neighboring farm had "stole the wagon and two horses ... then onto Col. Morgans, took off 10 of his negroes, and put off to Winchester, wagon loaded up with bedsteads and every sort of thing."[19] In August, there occurred "a grand stampede of negroes from the neighbourhood [sic], ten from the Hall, seven from the Meadow, two from the Briars, and one of ours."[20] Local concerns about whether slave forces would remain in place intensified greatly after January 1863, when Union General Robert H. Milroy established headquarters in the nearby town of Winchester. Indeed, for slave-holders of Clarke County, Milroy's control of Winchester and the surrounding countryside marked a turning point in the war, for he was determined to free slaves within the areas he controlled and thereby bring fully to fruition Lincoln's Emancipation Proclamation.[21]

In the early months of 1863, Milroy's troops scoured the countryside of Clarke County, taking slaves away from farms or identifying slaves to be taken later. Rarely was the departure of slaves from a farm a sudden, once-and-done event; rather, the process was episodic and gradual. In some cases, soldiers took only slaves who wanted to leave, which often meant that at least some remained while others departed, in consequence of which troops would later revisit the farm to take away slaves who might have reconsidered and decided to leave after all. Also, because members of slave families were often spread across numerous farms, with husbands on one farm and wives and children elsewhere, Milroy's soldiers sometimes appeared at farmhouses seeking specific women and children, apparently at the behest of their husbands and fathers. Once they had been transported to Winchester as refugees, emancipated slaves were expected to support themselves, which often resulted in members of slave families remaining separated from one another longer than might otherwise have been the case under the new conditions of freedom. In February of 1863, for example, Mattella Harrison wrote that one of her slaves had

---

[19] Kimball Diary, January 27, 1863.
[20] Mattella Harrison, "Civil War Diary of Mattella Harrison of Clarke County, Virginia, 1835-1898," *Proceedings of the Clarke County Historical Association*, 22 (1982-1983): 18.
[21] A useful discussion of Milroy's policies and the activities of his men in Winchester and its nearby environs may be found in Jonathan A. Noyalas, *"My Will is Absolute Law": A Biography of Union General Robert H. Milroy* (Jefferson, NC: McFarland Company, Inc., 2006), 79-105.

gone "up to Winchester to try to get his son Ben to return. He had a long talk with Milroy who informed him he would have to support his own family. The government would only transport them from the land of oppression. Hearing this, old Uncle Billy sent Aunt Nelly word she had best stay where she was as he could not transport the whole family, and if he could make any arrangements by which he could return, he would do so."[22]

February and March of 1863 marked the high tide of forced slave removals in Clarke County, and accounts of Milroy's troops carrying out what Harrison derisively referred to as "negro stealing expeditions" during those months are legion.[23] On February 2, Harrison wrote that "our tyrants in Winchester are drawing the reins tighter. They have carried off forcibly the servants in several places."[24] Widespread slave removals led to the growing intractability of slaves, causing women to complain about the "impudent and insolent" behavior of "lazy negroes."[25] One woman's husband, writing to her from his military encampment, noted that "it must be awful to submit to Negro and Yankee oppression both."[26] Anxiety stemming from the prospect of losing her slaves prompted Harrison to write a whistling-in-the-dark justification of slavery in which she explained the "superior civilization and refinements of the South, resulting from... slavery [: In] the relative position of master and slave from the time a child is old enough to be called master by his little dusky playmates, he feels himself in some measure the protector. It is his privilege to bestow good things, to benefit them in a thousand ways. He is taught the meanness of domineering or ill treatment of those who cannot retaliate and to love them for their very state of dependence. Thus all the finer feelings are called into play."[27] Harrison expressed alarm over additional instances of slave removals in her neighborhood, but remarked that her own slaves remained "composed" and were

[22] Harrison, "Civil War Diary," 40 (quotation), and 62.
[23] Ibid., 45.
[24] Ibid., 34.
[25] Daniel C. Snyder, Camp of 11th Reg't Va. Cav., near Harrisonburg, to Rachel (Louthan) Snyder, Berryville, VA, March 29, 1863, in Snyder Letters. See Faust, *Mothers of Invention*, 61, for a discussion of slaves' "diminishing motivation for work or obedience," as the Civil War progressed.
[26] Ibid.
[27] Harrison, "Civil War Diary," 41.

"behaving comparatively well."[28]

Subsequently, however, Harrison would be disheartened to learn that her slaves did not share her view of slavery. In late March of 1863 she recorded her dismay that one of her slaves had absconded to Winchester with the proceeds of five barrels of flour. She "felt not so much grieved at the loss as at the miserable ingratitude and treachery of one I had thought so upright and honest and had depended on and trusted." A few days later, Milroy's men arrived to "take all [slaves] who wanted to go." Some stayed but four departed, prompting her to lament that "those I had known from my childhood broke all ties as carelessly as if formed the day before."[29]

In tones of astonishment, anxiety, and sometimes anger, women bemoaned the disloyalty of their slaves. Some were stunned both by their slaves' decisions to leave and by their disrespectful behavior as they departed. Mary Etchison, for example, reported that "some of our servants acted very meanly before their departure, and I can never forget it for there was not the least necessity for it."[30] Similarly, Matella Harrison, after noting in her diary that her cousin had drawn "a tremendous tirade on herself by bidding [her servant] Jane goodbye," resolved that when Milroy's troops came for her own slaves she would not "show [herself or] give the servants a chance to insult" her.[31] Lucy Allen, anticipating the day when her slaves would be removed, resolved to "be cool and calm." When finally a soldier did come calling for one of her slaves, she met him with poise and equanimity until "he demanded meat for them," after which she "made [herself] a perfect fury."[32]

As news of slave removals circulated through the neighborhoods of rural Clarke, women engaged in the wishful thinking that Milroy's slave hunters, somehow, would miss their farms. Eventually, however, they resigned themselves to the reality that soon their slaves would be gone, and they began to reflect upon the circumstances by which their own slaves might soon flee or be

---

[28] Harrison, "Civil War Diary,", 41, 43.

[29] Ibid., 46, 48.

[30] Mary Elizabeth (Louthan) Etchison, Berryville, VA, to Carter Louthan, 25 May 1863, in Louthan Family Papers, Virginia Historical Society, Richmond, VA.

[31] Harrison, "Civil War Diary," 40.

[32] Lucy Allen, "Diary of Miss Lucy Allen of 'Clifton,'" *Proceedings of the Clarke County Historical Association*, 9 (1949): 28.

taken by Union troops, and upon how their own lives would change afterwards. In March of 1863, with federal troops encamped nearby, Lucy Allen suspected that the departure of her personal maid was imminent: "Tonight went to my room, found everything arranged as usual, fire made, dressing gown and slippers ready, but no maid ... but in the morning at a very late hour she made her appearance with some trivial excuse." The following day, Allen wrote that she had awoken that day "with the uncomfortable thoughts of having to dress in a cold room without fire, and to be my own handmaid, and to make my bed, clean up my room, in fact to take Louisa's place generally—but to my astonishment [she] made her appearance, tho at a later hour than usual, with an excuse I was compelled to take, without questioning too closely."[33] A few days later, when a federal cavalryman appeared under Allen's bedroom window demanding "this woman's children and clothes," she fulminated about the "deceit" and "ingratitude [of] the African race," before reflecting about the meaning of this event for her own life: "'twas not very pleasant to come to my room to night and find no fire kindled or none of the usual arrangements, but I will get used to being my own handmaid."[34]

As Mattella Harrison's slaves were leaving her, she tried her hand at making soap for the first time in her life and began to make a garden.[35] But even as she became more active in performing chores around her household, she preserved time for engaging in leisure activities that had marked her days in earlier times. One day in early May of 1863, for example, she mended some clothing and then worked in the garden before reading French until dinner, after which she returned to the garden to plant cantaloupes.[36] In reflecting upon her life without slaves, Harrison "felt intensely miserable," but claimed not to be concerned about "the pecuniary or loss of comfort." Rather, what troubled her most was that her husband would have to work so hard to provide "all the comforts" she knew he would want her to have. She also thought that in the future "many fewer [things would be] necessary for [her] comfort and happiness."[37]

---

[33] Allen, "Diary of Miss Lucy Allen," 26.
[34] Ibid., 28.
[35] Harrison, "Civil War Diary," 19, 50.
[36] Ibid., 56.
[37] Ibid., 54, 62.

Rachel Snyder abandoned farming altogether. After her slaves left and she could not find a white girl to take into her household, nor a "white boy to keep [her] in wood and work a garden," she sold her crops, livestock, and household goods at public auction and made plans to return to her ancestral home to live with her parents and sisters.[38] Meanwhile, important changes were afoot in that household. By late May of 1863, the 17 slaves that her father owned prior to the war were gone, and women of his household—his wife and daughters—were adjusting to life without them. They had hired a "white girl" but they were also learning to work. Mary Etchison, one of Louthan's daughters, described in a letter to her brother how they were adjusting to the "fate" shared by "almost every family": "A great many changes have taken place since you left home... you would hardly know us... each of us has our work to do and by that means we get through... the time has come near that we will all have to learn to work. The girls don't talk about much else now, but about domestic affairs." Then, after describing, with some humor, the poor results of her efforts to bake bread, she remarked that "I have been compelled to do many things lately that would surprise you very much. I thought at one time that perhaps I would have to go to cutting wood [and] I have been obliged to... milk cows." Notably, in these passages Etchison describes the "hard work" that "Clarke Ladies [now] enter into ... so willingly," as an effort to preserve leisure: "I think when we become accustomed to [work], that we will have almost as much leisure as we have always had."[39]

Etchison's prideful account of how she and the other women of her household were, with apparent equanimity, learning to do work that formerly had been performed by slaves should be read as a significant shift in the gender roles of white farm women. In the midst of the Civil War, fully two years before Appomattox, at least some women of Clarke showed a propensity for positioning themselves in gendered and racially defined work-space that formerly had been occupied by men and slaves. Women who had

---

[38] Daniel C. Snyder to Rachel (Louthan) Snyder, March 29, 1863; Mary Elizabeth (Louthan) Etchison to Carter Louthan, May 25, 1863, Louthan Family Papers, Virginia Historical Society, Richmond, VA.
[39] Mary Elizabeth (Louthan) Etchison to Carter Louthan, May 25, 1863, in ibid.

led lives of comfort and privilege enabled by a dependence on slave labor now embraced work as one aspect of their new lot in life without slaves. Whereas formerly they had spent their days reading, studying French, arranging flowers, visiting neighbors, and maintaining diaries and writing letters, they now cooked and baked bread, washed clothing, milked cows, made soap, kept gardens, and the like. But their new receptiveness to work routines, driven by necessity, also entailed an effort to conserve genteel forms of leisure, a key dimension of their lifestyles prior to the war. Thus, in an interpretive framework that dichotomizes women's behaviors and experiences as either embracing new conceptions of gender roles or recoiling from them, the farm women of Clarke County occupy middle ground.

The Bridge Blunder Before the Battle
Investigating the Shields-Carroll Controversy at Port Republic

Gary L. Ecelbarger

"The whole affair has been a stupendous blunder," groaned an Indiana captain a few days after the Battle of Port Republic. Another Hoosier officer redundantly ranted: "The responsible general should have his head decapitated."[40] The ire of the combat soldiers flew in two directions. Brigadier General James Shields, the division commander of the Port Republic force and Colonel Samuel Sprigg Carroll, one of Shields's brigade commanders, took the brunt of the criticism for their decisions in the action of June 8-9, 1862, where more than 1,000 U.S. soldiers were killed, wounded, and captured in or near the Shenandoah Valley hamlet of Port Republic. The commanders fueled the fire by pointing accusing fingers at each other. Brigadier General Erastus B. Tyler, directly commanding the two Union brigades that lost at Port Republic, also came under fire for fighting the battle in the first place.

A single issue stood out as the focal point of the argument. Colonel Carroll surprised Major General Thomas J. "Stonewall" Jackson when he led 150 Union cavalry and a section of artillery (both were a detachment from Shields's division) into Port Republic on the morning of June 8, 1862. The town served as Jackson's headquarters and his supply depot for his army's wagons. Jackson and most of his staff officers escaped from the town by riding across the bridge spanning the North River—the only way to cross this booming waterway. Carroll placed one cannon at the edge of the bridge, pointing it across the span toward Jackson's army while the other gun pointed southward as Union horse soldiers scurried to gain control of Port Republic.

With Jackson and his army on the north side of the river, separated by a mile from his wagons that were now within striking

---

[40] Elijah H. C. Cavins to his wife, June 12, 1862, Cavens Manuscript, Indiana Historical Society, Indianapolis, IN; O.T. to the editor, June 11, 1862, published in the *Indianapolis Journal*, June 19, 1862.

distance of Union troops teeming through the town, Colonel Carroll potentially controlled the fate of Jackson's army. If he burned the bridge, the Confederate wagons would belong to Shields's division and Jackson would be forced to fight against two Union armies—the Mountain Department under Major General John C. Frémont and the Department of the Rappahannock under Major General Irvin McDowell—without supplies. But Carroll refused to burn the bridge, later citing that his orders from General Shields (commanding a division in McDowell's army) explicitly instructed him to save it. Within half an hour, Stonewall Jackson retook the bridge and subsequently beat Frémont's and Shields's vanguard forces in twin victories at the battles of Cross Keys (June 8) and Port Republic (June 9).

The bridge incident contributed to shelving General Shields while also tarnishing the reputation of Colonel Carroll; each claimed he was wronged by the actions of the other. The participants debated for fifty years after the battle. Did General Shields order Colonel Carroll to save the bridge over the North River or to burn it on June 8, 1862? The *National Tribune* served as the preferred sounding board for partisans of Carroll and Shields to spar against each other over this issue. "History, so far as I know, has failed to tell who was responsible for that great blunder," insisted one of the early contributors to the Union veteran paper. "There are volumes of unwritten history stored in the minds of our comrades that should be given to the public before they are forever sealed."[41]

More than one dozen Union veterans did indeed release the history stored in their minds; this included three of Carroll's former staff officers. While their testimonies contributed mightily to the history of the campaign, they only muddied the turbid waters surrounding the bridge incident to leave this question unresolved. Modern interpretations have universally exonerated Carroll, nearly all pointing to a published dispatch Shields wrote to him on June 4 that ordered Carroll to save the bridge. Still, the affair has remained nebulous for authors and historians unsure of the exact destination of Shields's division as it advanced through the Luray Valley (that portion of the Shenandoah Valley bordered by the fifty-five-mile-long Massanutten Mountain range on the west and the Blue Ridge chain on the east) in the first week of June 1862.

---

[41] W. J. Brown to the editor, *National Tribune*, June 2, 1887.

Newly discovered documents at the National Archives force a reinvestigation of this issue. Red-stamped with "Copied, War Records, 1861-1865," but never published, these overlooked gems provide precious insight into Union command decisions in the Shenandoah Valley in June 1862. When these documents are spliced into a chronological timeline along with other archival and published dispatches and letters, the resulting paper trail leads to a revised and solidly documented interpretation of the Union advance to Port Republic.

The key to this understanding lies within the chronology. Rather than placing the dispatches in the order in which they were written, command decisions are better appreciated when the documents are placed in the order they are actually received by the intended recipients, particularly General Shields, the commander who directed the Union advance. This organizational technique yields a plan that changed three times in five days. It also highlights promises to subordinates that could not be kept while at the same time focuses in on a subordinate who was not up to the ever-evolving mission placed before him, particularly when three sets of orders relating to three different bridges wound up in his hands. In addition, we find that the denouement of Shields's division at Port Republic would never had happened if General Shields had received his orders from the U.S. War Department in a timely fashion. All of this reinterprets the counter campaign against Stonewall Jackson in the Shenandoah Valley.

The Union campaign for Port Republic commenced on the evening of June 1, 1862. Two days earlier, on May 30, 1862, the division of Brigadier General James Shields reentered the Shenandoah Valley and seized Front Royal after a brief engagement with the Confederate force stationed there. In doing so they recaptured most of the materiel that had originally fallen into Stonewall Jackson's hands one week earlier in his successful campaign against Major General Nathaniel P. Banks. In addition, 150 Confederate soldiers were led away as prisoners of war. The men in Shields's division had seen only victories in all of their skirmishes and battles, and had marched 300 miles in eighteen days. But their hard marching was about to enter a new tortuous phase and their string of victories—along with their existence—would soon come to an end.

"I have an important work for you to perform," wrote

General Shields to Colonel Samuel Sprigg Carroll, commander of his fourth brigade. Shields penned the dispatch at 8:00 P.M. on June 1, instructing Carroll to push southward from his camp near Front Royal at 4:00 the following morning with a select force of cavalry, artillery, and infantry. Carroll's mission was to advance deep into the Luray Valley to a hamlet called Conrad's Store. Once at his destination, Carroll was to burn Miller's Bridge, the span across the South Fork of the Shenandoah River that connected Conrad's Store with the road leading to Harrisonburg. "Jackson must be taken," continued Shields to Carroll, "The burning of the bridge will effect it."

At this hour Shields was convinced that Jackson—who was currently leading his harried army toward Woodstock—would attempt a crossing at Miller's Bridge in an effort to rush eastward past Conrad's Store and through Swift Run Gap in the Blue Ridge to an important supply depot at Stanardsville. Shields ordered Carroll to pass the other Shenandoah bridge crossings during his forty-five-mile mission. Shields determined to lead the bulk of his division to Columbia Bridge, eight miles southwest of Luray, where he planned to personally cross his brigades and smash Jackson's retreating force in the flank and rear. If Carroll cut off Jackson's escape route, then the Southern force would be trapped. "Everything depends on speed," wrote Shields to Carroll, closing his orders to the subordinate with a promise of a reward: "You will earn your star if you do all this."[42]

Shields planned on the night of June 1, 1862, to use the South Fork of the Shenandoah as a moat. The available maps of the period were crude, but they were accurate enough to inform Shields that three bridges spanned the river south of Front Royal. These were White House Bridge, four miles southwest of Luray; Columbia Bridge, eight miles upriver (meaning "south of" in Valley parlance) from there; and Miller's Bridge at Conrad's Store. A fourth bridge, called Red Bridge by the locals, was located between Miller's Bridge

---

[42] Shields to Carroll, June 1, 1862, in U.S. War Department (comp.), *War of the Rebellion: A Compilation of the Official Records of the Union and Confederate* Armies (Washington, D.C.: U.S. Government Printing Office, 1880-1901), ser. 1, vol. 12, pt. 3, 16-17 (hereafter cited as *OR*). Conrad's Store has been renamed "Elkton." Shields never identifies Miller's Bridge, but clearly refers to it in his instructions "to burn the bridge across the Shenandoah near Conrad's Store, on the road leading from Harrisonburg to Stanardsville." The abutments of the original still stand just north of the present bridge site.

and Columbia Bridge, but Confederate forces succeeded in burning that span two months earlier. Shields was well acquainted with White House Bridge, which he crossed less than three weeks earlier. He may have used an 1859 map of the Virginia region for his information about Miller's Bridge. The map is poor, but it clearly shows the bridge, naming it "Conrod's Bridge."

By omission it seems that Shields believed there was no other crossing for Jackson to use unless he advanced his Southerners twenty-five miles deeper in the Valley to head out eastward from Staunton through Waynesboro, two towns with depots on the Virginia Central Railroad. More likely, Shields maintained, is that Jackson would attempt to repeat his march through New Market Gap (he did this in his successful campaign to Front Royal two weeks earlier). But Shields planned to beat him to the two bridges that would deliver Jackson and his men into the Luray Valley. If Jackson chose to head to Staunton, then Shields would cross his available brigades and flank him at New Market. The plan's fault lay in numbers. Shields had three brigades to guard two bridges; he knew this was not enough. After he handed Carroll's instructions to a staffer, Shields wrote to his superior, Major General Irvin McDowell, commanding the Department of the Rappahannock, requesting reinforcements to Luray to aid in blocking Jackson's retreat route.[43]

Shields arose before dawn's first light on June 2. But the day came without the sun as torrents of rain covered the floor of the valley like a glossy sheet. The River Road from Front Royal to Luray was macadamized, but Jackson's cartographer, Jedediah Hotchkiss made careful note on one of his maps that this road was only decent in dry weather. Shields fretted in the early stages of his advance. Carroll had begun his mission on time and was off to Conrad's Store. But Shields's own trains plodded so slowly that he abandoned the notion that reinforcements would help him. "For God's sake let us have supplies instead of men," he exclaimed to McDowell's chief of staff, an efficient colonel named Edward Schriver. He also planted the idea to Schriver that the campaign should head in another direction. "Why not meet me at Gordonsville, turning all back to Fredericksburg to move on Richmond?" It appears at this moment Shields regretted being sent

---

[43] Shields to Colonel [Edward] Schriver, June 1, 1862, *OR* ser. 1, vol. 12, pt. 3, 315-16.

back to the Valley.[44]

Shields continued to press the idea of abandoning this new campaign even in its first day. He wrote to Secretary of War Edwin Stanton while on his way to Luray. Complaining about too many men and too few supplies— "Here now the men will starve"— Shields's petulance spilled over to the other side of the Massanutten when he fingered Major General John C. Frémont as the reason for Jackson's escape through Strasburg. "His [Frémont's] failure has saved Jackson," Shields complained. But Shields's intent was for Stanton to change his direction. "My dear friend, see the President," continued Shields. "Tell him that my opinion is to put things back again where they were as soon as possible. Bring Frémont's force... to Strasburg, Banks to Front Royal, McDowell again to Fredericksburg, where I can join him, and we will hurl them out of Richmond as fast as we can march."[45]

Union cavalry passed through Luray and trotted westward out to White House Bridge on the evening of June 2. Shields learned that he must alter his plans. Jackson's cavalry had burned both White House Bridge and Columbia Bridge hours before the Union arrival. Hearing Frémont's cannons trace southward, "up" the Valley Turnpike, Shields deduced that Jackson was trying to escape. Unyielding rains continued to swell the South Fork of the Shenandoah River, now a formidable obstacle separating forces in the Valley. Shields ordered his engineers to construct a pontoon over the river, swollen with swift waters running twelve feet deep. By 4:00 the following morning he had not given up. "We must cross to-day somehow," he declared. He believed his only option was to try to run Jackson down, since the wily Confederate had turned the tables on him.[46]

Frustrated in a several-hour effort to cross the irksome river, Shields entertained the notion to push his entire four-brigade force to Conrad's Store. He had yet to hear from Colonel Carroll, who he had ordered to burn the bridge there. Now he wished that bridge to be saved, but it would be unnecessary to countermand his orders to his subordinate. "The bridge [at Conrad's Store] I expect to find burned also," wrote Shields to McDowell at 10:30 A.M. on June 3, "but

---

[44] Jedediah Hotchkiss Sketchbook, Library of Congress, Washington, D.C.; Shields to Schriver, June 2, 1862, OR ser. I, vol. 12, pt. 3, 321.
[45] Shields to Stanton, June 2, 1862, OR ser. I, vol. 12, pt. 3, 322.
[46] Shields to General McDowell, June 3, 1862, in ibid., 326.

by going higher up we may find a ford. This would bring us out at Harrisonburg." By specifically planning to seek a ford, Shields had revealed on June 3 that he did not know of the existence of the bridge over the North River at Port Republic.[47]

Shields correctly predicted the fate of Miller's Bridge. Captain Samuel Coyner of the 7th Virginia Cavalry burned the bridge during the early morning hours of June 3. The rain had let up enough for the bridge to kindle. "Soon the bridge was on fire," wrote Coyner to his sister, "and then Providence intervened; the windows of Heaven opened, the floods came and Jackson was safe."[48] Little did Coyner realize that his mission at Miller's Bridge was wholly unnecessary, for Colonel Carroll would have burned the bridge anyway if he beat Coyner there to satisfy his now-outdated June 1 order. Carroll and his command had been so slowed by the abominable roads south of Luray that he did not reach Miller's Bridge until 5:00 A.M. on June 4—exactly twenty-four hours after Coyner burned it. Carroll sent a dispatch to be carried twenty miles back to Shields, ostensibly describing his odyssey on impassible roads.[49]

Approximately one mile east of Columbia Bridge, at the hamlet of Alma, Shields established his headquarters. He must have already assessed the problematic roads prior to receiving Carroll's dispatch. This forced him to continue the option of trying to pontoon the river near the felled bridge. Once he received confirmation from Carroll, Shields scrawled a message to be delivered to General McDowell. "You will perceive from this and my previous communications that all the bridges . . . have been destroyed. Owing to the recent heavy rains the river has become so swollen as to make a crossing impossible for the present. The roads have become impassible for wagons beyond Columbia Bridge. We cannot fight against the elements. . . To fall back would not better our condition, as there is nothing at Front Royal, and it might lead to a stampede of this whole army." Indeed, Shields felt stuck in the mud.[50]

But Shields exhibited an entire change of demeanor and

---

[47] Shields to McDowell, June 3, 1862, *OR* ser. 1, vol. 12, pt. 3, 325.
[48] Samuel B. Coyner to his sister, June 5, 1862, Coyner Papers, Augusta County Historical Society, Staunton, VA.
[49] Shields to McDowell, June 4, 1862, *OR* ser. 1, vol. 12, pt. 3, 335.
[50] Ibid.

outlook by the evening of June 4. Sometime during the afternoon he learned that an intact bridge spanned the North River at Port Republic. (The North and South Rivers surrounded the Port and converged at the southeast corner of the town to form the South Fork of the Shenandoah.) This bridge offered Shields new life and a new mission. He may have learned of the bridge from citizens near Luray or from a dispatch Carroll sent him. South River could be crossed at a ford (this river was the smallest and shallowest of the two tributaries), but Pirkey's Ford over North River was a more hazardous crossing, particularly when the river boomed as it did in June of 1862. Therefore, the bridge over the North River, one mile downriver from the ford and 150 yards upriver from the confluence of the North and South Rivers, offered the only reasonable avenue for twenty miles for an army to pass across the South Fork of the Shenandoah and its tributaries.

Shields immediately fired off instructions to Colonel Joseph Thoburn, who held the rest of Carroll's brigade two miles southeast of Columbia Bridge. Thoburn was ordered to take his command, advance through the mud, and join Carroll at Conrad's Store. "There is no time for delay," warned Shields in his order, "This is the time to be men." Shields then followed up with new instructions for Carroll. "The whole of your command is to march to join you," Shields promised, exhorting Carroll to head to Staunton and destroy all the cars and facilities at the railroad depot there to prevent Jackson's escape eastward. The last line of Shields's dispatch to Carroll of June 4 set the stage for a controversy that would fester into the next century: "You must go forward at once with cavalry and guns to save the bridge at Port Republic."[51]

Twenty-four hours after writing these new instructions, Shields learned that his plans must change again. An orderly from Carroll arrived at Alma during the evening of June 5. The dispatch he passed on to Shields has never come to light, but based on Shields's response to Carroll and subsequent dispatches received and returned, it appears that Carroll's scouts informed him that the Port Republic bridge was out, downed five weeks earlier by Confederate forces. This intelligence, however, was completely

---

[51] Thoburn to Carroll, June 5, 1862 & Shields to Thoburn, June 4, 1862, 12th Army Corps Papers, RG 393, National Archives, Washington, D.C. (Hereafter cited as NA; all references to National Archive sources refer to RG 393); Shields to Carroll, June 4, 1862, OR ser. 1, vol. 12, pt. 3, 335.

erroneous.

Carroll ostensibly passed along the misinformation in his June 5 dispatch to Shields, who altered his plans based on this error. "I have received your very instructive communication, and kept the orderly until this morning," came Shields's reply written at 11:00 A.M. on June 6. Informing Carroll that the rest of his brigade was on its way to join him, Shields asked, "Can you prepare for a spring on Waynesborough [sic] to burn the bridge, depot, cars, and tear up the railroad? Will this be practicable? I fear the enemy will escape if it

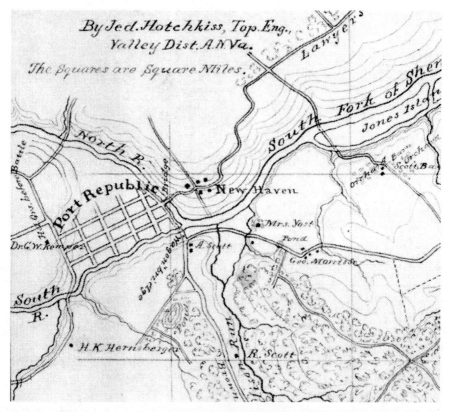

Detail of map drawn by Jedediah Hotchkiss showing Port Republic and bridge over North River (Library of Congress, Geography and Map Division)

is not done."[52]

Essentially, Shields wished Carroll to perform the same mission he had in mind back on the evening of June 4. But the depot destruction no longer was to occur at Staunton. Now the destination was Waynesboro, a depot town nineteen miles south of Port Republic, which did not require a major river crossing. "If you can cut the road at Waynesborough [sic] it will be a splendid exploit, and end Jackson," Shields insisted.[53] Thus, General Shields suffered from the same faulty intelligence that hampered Union commanders in the Valley for two more years—the bridge at Waynesboro was made of iron, not wood.

In five days, Shields's plan evolved through three distinct destinies. He first intended to block Jackson at White House and Columbia Bridge (June 1-2), then he planned on beating him to the railroad depot at Staunton (June 4-5). This progressed quickly to a race for Waynesboro. Through it all, Shields had not given up on affecting a crossing at the site of Columbia Bridge. His perseverance paid off later on June 6 when his engineers announced that the pontoon was finished. This allowed Shields to communicate more directly with Frémont: messengers need only gallop nine miles through New Market Gap to link with Fremont versus the sixty-five miles required to ride around Signal Knob at Strasburg. During the evening of June 6, Shields sent cavalry and infantry across the makeshift bridge and through the gap to New Market.[54]

After making the communication, Shields attempted to push his command toward Conrad's Store. He found the roads utterly impassable—"Further no human effort could go." The wheels sunk in the mud to the axle, and the mountain torrents cut between portions of his command and separated them. He also heard (false) reports that General James Longstreet was leading a force of at least 8,000 men who threatened his position east of the Blue Ridge. Still stuck in the mud with dwindling supplies, Shields put two flourmills in Luray in operation to feed his men. Shields's

---

[52] Shields to Carroll, June 6, 1862, OR ser. 1, vol. 12, pt. 3, 349. On June 12, Shields wrote that Carroll reported that the bridge was burned five days ago. This would place the report at June 7 (Another Shields's letter claims "five weeks ago"). See OR ser. 1, vol. 12, pt. 3, 684, 686 to note the discrepancies. Based on Shields's immediate change of plans between June 4 and the morning of June 6, the faulty Carroll report must have been given to him no later than June 5.
[53] Shields to Carroll, June 6, 1862, in ibid., 349.
[54] Shields to Schriver, June 8, 1862, ibid., 358-61.

mills and incoming supplies sustained his men, but the number of barefoot soldiers rose into the thousands, and one brigade commander insisted that 200 of his soldiers had no pants. No additional infantry, including Carroll's fourth brigade, was moving to Carroll's support, despite Shields's assurance to the contrary to his subordinate.[55]

By the night of June 7, Shields had effectively exchanged information with Frémont across his pontoons. As Saturday disappeared with the midnight hour, Shields was aroused from his sleep by one of his orderlies to inform him that a message from Colonel Carroll had arrived. Written from Conrad's Store at 3:30 P.M., the dispatch announced that Carroll was on his way to Waynesboro with the possibility of bagging two Confederate supply trains—one coming in from Stanardsville and Jackson's train sitting at Port Republic. Carroll divulged that his scouts informed him that all of Jackson's trains idled at Port Republic, waiting for the river to fall to cross for Waynesboro. Complaining that his infantry commander (Colonel James Gavin of the 7th Indiana) was forced to leave 250 men behind for sickness as well as for want of shoes and socks, Carroll closed, "I will do all that man can do to get them either at Port Republic or Waynesboro. I will send you back a message from Port Republic."[56]

Carroll's dispatch indicates he still believed the bridge was out over the North River at Port Republic. His scouts also misled him or miscommunicated to him, for if Jackson's train was in Port Republic (and indeed it was), the supplies could roll to Waynesboro without having to cross a major waterway. Jackson's potential dilemma was that he separated the trains from his army, which bivouacked on the opposite side of the North River. But it is apparent from Carroll's dispatch that he believed the wagons were across the North River from Port Republic. Carroll had left at 4:00 P.M. on June 7 with no idea that a bridge stood between Jackson's army and his wagons.

Shields ranted the moment he received Carroll's dispatch. "Such is my anxiety that I rise from my bed to write to you," began

---

[55] Shields to Schriver, June 8, 1862, *OR* ser. 1, vol. 12, pt. 3, 358-361. For a revealing and trustworthy account of the missing pants and shoes of the division, see Nathan Kimball to Adj. General, March, 1864, Reports of the U.S. Army Generals, M1098, NA.

[56] Carroll to Shields, June 7, 1862, Shields Papers, U.S. Army Heritage and Educatioon Center, Carlisle, PA. (Hereafter cited as Shields Papers).

Shields's 2:00 A.M. reply on June 8. Convinced that Carroll could foil Jackson, even with a force smaller than a brigade, Shields blasted away at Carroll to urge him onward:

> The enemy has flung away everything; knapsacks and their stragglers fill the mountain. They only need a movement on the flank to panic-strike them, and break them into fragments. No man has had such a chance since the war commenced. Few men ever had such a chance. You are within 30 miles of a broken, retreating enemy, who still hangs together. . . This enemy insulted the capital of your country; he is in retreat; you are within a day and a half of him, and you hesitate. I don't mean you personally, but some of your officers and men. This would be a disgrace. Can this be my boasted Shields' division? If an officer hesitates, send him back. Go on with the men. [57]

Shields ended the dispatch by promising Carroll reinforcements. He ordered half of his infantry, Carroll's fourth brigade and Brigadier General Erastus B. Tyler's third brigade, to move off at 6:00 A.M. along with three artillery batteries. Shields's other two brigades, under Brigadier General Nathan Kimball and Brigadier General Orris Ferry, stayed in and near Luray. Shields's force was woefully strung out for twenty-five miles along soupy roads. This set-up for failure had passed the notice of the War Department and General McDowell, who had let Shields operate in the Luray Valley with little supervision, save for insisting that he keep his division as closed up as possible during his advance. The content of Shields's dispatches—particularly those to Carroll—were either briefly summarized for higher command or not mentioned at all.

Shields was extremely hampered by delayed responses delivered to him from General McDowell. Early in the morning of June 8 he received a rare dispatch from McDowell's chief of staff, but the message was dated June 5. The letter questioned Shields's ability to get his force to Staunton, obviously unaware that Shields's plans had switched to Waynesboro two days hence. While Shields

---

[57] Shields to Carroll, June [8], 1862, OR ser. 1, vol. 12, pt. 3, 352-53. Although Shields dated the dispatch June 7, it is clear he is responding to Carroll's unpublished dispatch; therefore, the date had to be June 8. It is common to see dispatches written within a few hours of midnight to be incorrectly dated to the previous day.

scribbled out a lengthy response for headquarters, probably between 8 and 9:00 A.M., three scouts from Frémont interrupted him to inform him about Jackson's change of plans. Elated by his intelligence coup, Shields's exuberance gushed out in his closing comments to Colonel Schriver:

> *General Frémont is at Harrisonburg; Jackson's rear guard 4 miles on the road to Staunton. The bridge across the North River, on the turnpike, has been burned by some of my cavalry. This has stopped their march on Staunton, and turned them on the road to Port Republic to escape by Waynesborough. The advance of my column near Port Republic report that the enemy's train is on the other side of the river waiting for the water to fall. I have let General Frémont know this, and sent orderlies to keep me informed. Thus you will see he is caught, if these suppositions and dispositions are all right. . .*
>
> *I go forward myself to-day with the two additional brigades, leaving Luray to be garrisoned by my shoeless men and inefficient until a force can join them from Front Royal. Please let the general know the position at once; he will see the necessity for sending on a few regiments as fast as they can be forwarded. I will keep him constantly advised of our operations. I think we will finish Jackson.[58]*

This bombastic closure numbered Shields's days as a division commander. By repeating Carroll's intelligence that Jackson's trains were "on the other side of the river waiting for the water to fall," Shields implied that he did not expect any bridge at or near Port Republic to be intact. Thus, Shields felt that Jackson was trapped from advancing over the North River into Port Republic, and that Colonel Carroll would block the trains. His last known written orders to Carroll about the Port Republic (North River) bridge was the June 4 order to save it. This fit nicely with his plan to head to Staunton. But since June 5, Shields had intended to get to Waynesboro. He never sent Carroll orders to burn the bridge at Port Republic because he and Carroll believed from June 5 that the

---

[58] Schriver to Shields, June 5, 1862 & Shields's response, June 8, 1862, *OR* ser. 1, vol. 12, pt. 3, 340, 358-61.

bridge there was already downed.

A recently discovered dispatch confirms this. Immediately after Shields closed his letter to Colonel Schriver (approximately 9:00 A.M.), he wrote to Colonel Carroll repeating the same intelligence he had just received from Frémont's three scouts. Believing that Jackson would try to cross the North River to enter Port Republic in an effort to head to Waynesboro, Shields left his most specific instructions for Carroll about what to do in the town. "The artillery must take position to defend the ford at Port Republic or wherever they may attempt to pass. The infantry support it. I will be with you soon." Shields expected Port Republic would be a brief interlude for Carroll. He further reminded Carroll to save the supplies at Waynesboro, but to burn the bridge (at Waynesboro) and do everything necessary "to prevent enemy's escape."[59] The ford Shields referred to appears to be Pirkey's Ford, upriver from the bridge. This was the lone passage Shields believed Jackson could use only when the booming North River dropped low enough to cross. Clearly, he wrote to Carroll believing the bridge was out.

He also wrote to Carroll believing that Jackson's trains were *across* the river from Port Republic and not on the Port side where they actually rested. Shields's misapprehension is clear from the dispatch he sent back with Frémont's scout. "I think by this time there will be twelve pieces of artillery opposite Jackson's train at Port Republic, if he has taken that route," wrote Shields to Frémont at 9:30 A.M., "Some cavalry and artillery have pushed on to Waynesborough [sic] to burn the bridge. I hope to have two brigades at Port Republic to-day." He went on to explain to Frémont that if Jackson "attempts to force a passage, . . . I hope you will thunder down on his rear." The "force a passage" reference dovetails well with Carroll's instructions to block the ford. This adds more evidence that Shields did not expect the bridge over the North River at Port Republic to be standing.[60]

Neither did Carroll, who had already been repulsed at Port Republic before Shields handed his dispatch off to Frémont's

---

[59] Shields to Carroll, June 8, 1862, NA.
[60] Shields to Frémont, June 8, 1862, *OR* ser. I, vol. 12, pt. I, 21-22. Although published, this dispatch is essentially hidden within the body of Fremont's twenty-four page report of his operations in the Shenandoah Valley and has rarely, if ever, been cited. It is important for revealing what Shields knew, but its 9:30 A.M. heading also helps arrange a time line for other dispatches Shields wrote that morning.

courier.[61] Carroll and his advance had stormed into Port Republic early in the morning of June 8 and nearly captured an unwary Stonewall Jackson. But Jackson escaped—over the intact bridge across the North River—leaving his wagons separated briefly from the bulk of his army. During the melee Carroll saw the bridge and may have been surprised at its existence. If he burned the structure, he would have effectively isolated Jackson's wagons and forced Jackson to remain east of the tributaries that formed the South Fork of the Shenandoah. He then could isolate the two companies of Confederate infantry and untested lone battery of artillery in Port Republic and eventually capture Jackson's wagons. This left the door open to head to Waynesboro and destroy the depot there. This had been Shields's mission since June 5.

For some odd reason, however, Carroll remained confused about his mission. Holding onto his outdated June 4 order to save the bridge, Carroll attempted to do just that, although he clearly left Conrad's Store sixteen hours earlier fully understanding that an existing bridge would foil the Waynesboro mission. He positioned two cannons in the town (one at the end of the bridge) and tried to collect prisoners in the town. But sufficient Confederate infantry and artillery rallied to overwhelm Carroll's tenuous and unsupported position. By midmorning, the Union force retreated over the ford of the South River, leaving both cannons and scores of wounded and captured behind. Jackson survived his closest scrape to date in the Civil War.[62]

Despite his insistence that he would join Carroll, Shields never left Alma during the daylight hours of June 8. No telegraph lines ran out to his position; therefore, all transmissions between his headquarters and McDowell's chief of staff in Front Royal continued to be carried by a courier on horseback. The costly delay produced a tremendous irony for this portion of the campaign. By the afternoon of June 8, the U.S. War Department in Washington transmitted two messages by wire—both dispatches left Front Royal on horseback to be delivered to Shields. His mission in the Valley was over, for Union high command was granting his wish to

---

[61] The dispatch may have been received by General Tyler the next morning (June 9) and was mentioned in his after-action report.

[62] For a detailed description of this action, see Robert K. Krick, *Conquering the Valley: Stonewall Jackson at Port Republic* (Baton Rouge: Louisiana State University Press, 1996), 39-112.

rejoin the campaign for Richmond. "Send immediately to Major-General Shields," wrote McDowell in closing to his chief of staff, "and direct him to call in his division and march, via Warrenton, to Fredericksburg, to resume our former operations." As soon as Shields received the message he was to suspend his operation in the Luray Valley, collect his force, and march to Warrenton.[63]

Shortly after 6:00 P.M. on June 8, Shields received a courier. The orderly was not carrying McDowell's orders, for he rode in from the south. This message was from Carroll, describing his setback at Port Republic nine hours earlier. Shields wrote four dispatches during the next hour. His first was sent to General Frémont. For the first time in four days, Shields mentioned the bridge at Port Republic, but was disingenuous about what he knew of it in his message to Frémont. "I pushed forward Colonel Carroll… to move on Port Republic to burn the bridge and check the advance of the enemy," Shields wrote in the first line of his dispatch. He created the impression that he sent Carroll to Port Republic to burn a bridge that he thought was already down.[64]

After updating Colonel Schriver, Shields wrote orders to General Tyler, ignorant of the fact that Tyler had already joined Carroll a little over two miles northeast of Port Republic and was weighing his options about battling Jackson the following morning. Shields finally responded to Colonel Carroll at 7:45 P.M. Shields announced: "Kimball's brigade is marching rapidly to your support. Ferry's brigade is also in motion. I hope we will soon be able to recover lost ground. I will be with you in the morning."[65]

This recently unearthed response to Colonel Carroll underscores Shields's propensity to mislead his subordinates. On several occasions he assured Carroll that he was on his way to support him when, in fact, he had barely budged from his Columbia Bridge position since arriving there six days earlier. Kimball was not "marching rapidly" to Carroll's support. He was moving to Stanardsville and would receive no orders to head to Conrad's Store

[63] Schriver to Shields, June 8, 1862 (2), *OR*, ser. I, vol. 12, pt. 3, 357-58.

[64] Shields to Fremont, June 8, 1862, *OR*, ser. I, vol. 12, pt. I, 23. This dispatch, like the one cited in ref. #23, is buried within Frémont's lengthy Valley report.

[65] Shields to Schriver, June 8, 1862, *OR* , ser. I, vol. 12, pt. I, p. 683; Shields to Carroll, June 8, 1862, NA. Shields letter to Frémont is mentioned in his cited dispatch to Schriver. In Tyler's after-action report, he acknowledged receiving Shields's orders, but not until June 9, "and while writing a reply, was informed that the enemy were advancing upon us." Tyler report, *OR,* ser. I, vol. 12, pt. I, 696.

until the morning of June 9. The same is true for General Ferry and his brigade near Luray. Had Kimball's brigade been given orders to march overnight toward Port Republic, he would have added four more regiments to the Union line by mid-morning of June 9. (General Kimball had efficiently conducted nighttime marches of similar distances earlier in the Valley Campaign). Given the length of the June 9 battle and Jackson's difficulties in overcoming the Union defense, four additional Union regiments could reasonably have influenced the outcome.[66]

Shields's unearthed dispatches may answer a puzzling question about the Battle of Port Republic, fought on June 9: Why did General Tyler choose to fight Jackson near the Coaling and wheat fields of the Lewis farm with only two depleted brigades totaling a mere 2,600 infantrymen? Since Shields assured Carroll that support was "marching rapidly" to join him, perhaps Tyler made his decision under the same misapprehension. It is noteworthy that Tyler did not receive Shields's June 8 dispatch, written at 7:15 P.M. until 6:00 the following morning.[67]

General Tyler adds a related historical mystery to his decision about fighting at Port Republic. Late in the afternoon or early evening of June 8, as Tyler and Carroll were deciding whether or not to attack Jackson's force that day, Tyler wrote in his report: "About this time your [Shields's] order to commandant of post at Port Republic was handed me. Upon it and the opinion of these officers I ordered the infantry back to bivouac for the night." Tyler likely referred to Shields's order to Carroll about defending the ford at Port Republic. Taken in context with the information Shields had at the time he crafted the order, it is clear that Shields referred to Pirkey's Ford in the North River in his dispatch. But Tyler was not privy to his commander's plans. It is quite possible that he interpreted Shields's order as one to defend the ford over the South River—a reasonable conclusion since no bridge ever existed there.[68]

An unearthed letter that Tyler wrote to his family lends support to the above hypothesis. "I was ordered there [Port Republic] by Gen. Shields to hold the position," explained Tyler to his father a week after the battle, "Although I saw at a glance I could

---

[66] Nathan Kimball's Report of the U.S. Army Generals, M1098, NA.
[67] Tyler report, *OR*, ser. I, vol. 12, pt. I, 695-96.
[68] Ibid.; Shields to Carroll, June 8, 1862, NA.

not do it, yet I determined not to give it up without a struggle." Since Tyler's scouts misinformed him at early light the morning of the battle that Jackson had not crossed the rivers, one can conclude that Tyler stayed near Port Republic with a mission to block the South River fords. This became a moot plan once Jackson surprised him before 6:00 A.M. with a large force firing upon Tyler's men from the Union side of the river.[69]

Shields finally budged from his position late on June 8, leading Ferry's brigade southward. Dawn's first light on June 9 found him ten miles north of Conrad's Store; this is where and when Colonel Schriver's courier from Front Royal caught up to him. There, for the first time, Shields learned that his division had been recalled to Fredericksburg—fifteen precious hours after those orders were crafted. Shields fired back an acknowledgement at 5:45 A.M.[70] and continued his advance to Conrad's Store, where he expected Tyler and Carroll to be held up in a defensive position. By the time he approached Conrad's Store, morning was waning to noon and Shields learned of the desperate fight the two leading brigades put up eight miles south of there. Tyler and Carroll fought well for more than four hours, inflicting 800 casualties upon Jackson's army. But Jackson's numbers proved overwhelming. The Union guns were captured and turned on them, forcing a hasty retreat. The result was 1,000 casualties—greater than one-third of the force engaged—most of them captured. This was the Battle of Port Republic, the final and most brutal contest in Stonewall Jackson's 1862 Shenandoah Valley Campaign.

A latter 20th century lesson teaches us that the worst in an individual is exposed not necessarily because of the mistakes that he makes, but in his effort to cover-up the errors of his way. It is here where General James Shields authored his own demise. He came back to the Valley in June of 1862 with a record of trying to change history to his favor. This happened three months earlier in the aftermath of the First Battle of Kernstown. Shields, incapacitated with a broken arm in Winchester during the ten-hour fight, issued no orders for the contest on March 23, 1862. Nathan Kimball won the

---

[69] Tyler to his father, June 17, 1862, published in the (New Castle, PA) *Lawrence Journal* on June 28, 1862. Tyler's father lived in New Castle; he provided the letter to the editor of the paper to publish for his readers.
[70] Shields to Schriver, June 9, 1862, NA. The same dispatch is published in the Official Records, but without the time (5:45 A.M.) placed on it. See *OR*, ser. 1, vol. 12, pt. 3, 365.

battle, beating Stonewall Jackson for the only time in his independent career. But Shields's report claimed otherwise. He maintained that he called all the shots from his sickbed and that Kimball merely relayed his instructions. Predictably, Kimball and his allies fumed at Shields's vainglorious display and somehow convinced the Joint Committee on the Conduct of the War to investigate this Union victory. The seven-member body held a hearing on May 22 where four witnesses embarrassed Shields with their testimony that revealed he had no idea a battle was even occurring at Kernstown until the mid-afternoon of March 23. So Shields returned to the Valley during the last days of May leading a command of suspicious subordinates and superiors more closely inspecting every word he spoke or wrote.[71]

Perhaps Shields was aware of the heightened scrutiny. He had been laboring behind the scenes for a military promotion from brigadier to major general. Hailed as a hero after Kernstown, Shields was rapidly dropping out of favor with his angry junior officers. He also learned later on June 9 that General McDowell, who was still unaware of the battle that morning, openly criticized him for sending "a part of your force so far ahead that it could have no support." McDowell had earlier sent instructions to keep Shields's force together as it advanced up the Luray Valley. Shields decided not to inform his superiors about the Port Republic battle until the following morning.[72]

As the sun rose on June 10, Shields sheepishly reported on his division's loss at Port Republic, seventeen hours after he learned of its results. Here the excuses began: "We [General Frémont and Shields] expected to join forces and attack the enemy, but for the preemptory orders to return," Shields claimed. He then tried to write off the separation of his forces as the result of the unpredicted rains, failing to mention that he continued to string out the forces for days during the daily torrents. When Colonel Schriver got his hands on Shields's letter later that day, he wired it to McDowell while writing beneath Shields's words, "The above is a sorry picture of Shields' division... There is nothing but confusion and

---

[71] Third Session of the 39th Congress, *Report of the Joint Committee of the Senate on the Conduct of the War*, (Washington, D.C.: Government Printing Office, 1863), vol. 3, pt. 2, 403-14.
[72] Colonel Schriver to Shields, June 9, 1862, *OR*, ser. I, vol. 12, pt. 3, 364.

disorder."[73]

Shields refused to take any responsibility for his division's mismanagement in the Luray Valley. He cited Carroll for neglecting to burn the North River bridge, although he was incorrect on the length of time Carroll actually had possession of the span: "His [Carroll's] report to me that the bridge was burned five weeks ago deceived me. He held it three-quarters of an hour, and wanted the good sense to burn it." Shields then took a shot at Carroll and Tyler: "They took up an indefensible position afterward instead of a defensible one. But notwithstanding all these blunders the men behaved nobly." In a private letter to the Secretary of War, Shields ranted about Carroll's and Tyler's "foolish" performance.[74] As it turned out, the ground was defensible at the Port Republic battle site, proven by the stalwart defense Tyler and Carroll offered for more than four hours. What made it indefensible was the lack of supporting regiments Shields had promised several days before. But those orders never left Shields's headquarters, even though he assured Colonel Carroll (and likely General Tyler) that support was swiftly on its way.

In the flurry of dispatches referring to this campaign that were collected for publication in the Official Records is a most curious one that has survived for posterity:

HEADQUARTERS SHIELDS' DIVISION,

Front Royal, Va., June 4, 1862.

Capt. E. B. OLMS[T]ED:

SIR: You are directed to send a detail of forty pioneers with a lieutenant to accompany the command under Colonel Carroll to Port Republic. Be particular to instruct your men to burn the bridge at that place.

---

[73] Shields to Schriver, June 10, 1862, embodies in report of Schriver to McDowell, *OR*, ser. 1, vol. 12, pt. 3, 367-68. The time of Shields' dispatch is listed as 5:30 P.M., but was actually 5:30 A.M. See original version in RG 393, NA.
[74] Shields to Schriver, June 11, 1862, *OR*, ser. 1, vol. 12, pt. 3, 371-72; Shields to Secretary Stanton, June 13, 1862, Stanton Papers, Library of Congress, Washington, D.C.

I am, captain, very respectfully,

J. R. SWIGART,
Lieutenant of Volunteers and Actg. Asst. Adjt. Gen.[75]

The June 4 order, cited above, gives specific orders from Shields to burn the bridge at Port Republic. Careful scrutiny raises suspicions that this is an after-the-fact fabricated instruction. On June 4, Shields had issued direct orders for Carroll to save the bridge, not to burn it. (Shields's objective at this date was Staunton—why would he burn his only remaining crossing to get there?). The dispatch heading also is erroneous. Shields's headquarters was not Front Royal on June 4; it was thirty miles south of it at Alma, near Columbia Bridge. Lieutenant J. R. Swigart, the author of the note in question, was Kimball's assistant adjutant general and was also nowhere near Front Royal at this time. Did Shields or his supporters submit this order to cover up the fiasco at the bridge? The answer may never be known, but it is clear that everything associated with the instruction was inconsistent with Shields's mission and location on June 4, 1862.[76]

Colonel Samuel S. Carroll, also looking for a promotion, could see his name being dragged through the mud and refused to be made a scapegoat for the Port Republic bridge fiasco. He took temporary leave of his command, rode out to Washington, and apparently found an audience with superior officers at the War Department. He submitted eight dispatches written by Shields to him, building the case that Shields's only instruction concerning the bridge at Port Republic was the June 4 order to save it.[77]

The series of dispatches, filed in McDowell's papers in an envelope marked "Gen. Shields' orders to Col. Carroll," influenced the collapse of Shields's military career. They lay out a strong case that Shields misled his subordinates and never

---

[75] *OR,* ser. I, vol. 51, pt. I, 95.
[76] Compare ref. #36 side by side with order of same date to Carroll in *OR,* ser. I, vol. 12, pt. 3, 335. A recent campaign study also considers the possibility of fabrication of this document. See Krick, *Conquering the Valley,* 61.
[77] General Shields's Orders to Colonel Carroll, RG 393, NA.

issued written orders for Carroll to burn the Port Republic bridge. Not only did Shields not win an additional star as major general, he was shelved by the War Department and never took the field again. His division was broken up and dispersed. Shields resigned his commission in 1863 and headed off to retirement in San Francisco.

Colonel Carroll was denied a brigadier general's commission, suggesting that the War Department held him at least partially culpable for his performance in the Port Republic campaign. Carroll proved himself an able officer for the Second Corps of the Army of the Potomac throughout the remainder of the war. Not only did he earn a brigadier's commission in 1864, he was breveted major general of volunteers by muster out in 1865. He returned to the U.S. Army and retired in 1869.[78]

The debate about the Port Republic bridge blunder lived as long as did the survivors of the action's participants. Veterans of the war divided themselves into Shields and Carroll camps and pressed their cases for decades after the guns of the Civil War fell silent. They could never settle the issue because it appears that both officers needed to shoulder the blame for Jackson's escape and subsequent victory at Port Republic. Carroll did indeed lack the good sense to burn the bridge—just as Shields claimed in the immediate aftermath—and should have realized that the June 4 order to save the bridge had been long outdated. Carroll knew his mission had changed; his June 7 acknowledgement that he (Carroll) was on his way to Waynesboro survives in Shields's personal papers today. It would have been folly for Carroll to leave that bridge intact as he headed south from it, for this assured that Jackson could attack him from behind.

General Shields is the lone source to implicate Carroll about misinforming his commander about the bridge. If Carroll never passed along any information about the bridge, then Shields is guilty of a cover-up. It should be noted, however, that Shields's insistence that Carroll inadvertently deceived him is reliable testimony, given the position of the forces and the date (June 5) that Shields received Carroll's courier. His day-old-plan to head to Staunton changed immediately to a drive for

---

[78] Samuel Sprigg Carroll Commission Branch File, M1064, NA.

Waynesboro; this modification appears to trace its origins to valuable information Carroll passed to Shields on the night of the 5th. That Shields believed the bridge was gone is certain, based on his subsequent words and actions. This makes Carroll as the most likely source of the erroneous intelligence, since the colonel was twenty-five miles closer to the disputed bridge.

General McDowell's leadership in the first ten days of June was detrimentally passive. He departed the Valley for Washington on June 6. He did little to tighten the reigns on his most active subordinate, General Shields, before or after this date. The paper trail that survives suggests that McDowell was generally oblivious to Shields's movements and his mission from June 5 onward. That Shields did not receive Colonel Schriver's June 5 dispatch until June 8 proves that McDowell was ignorant of Shields's change of plan that morphed from trying to cross the river to get to Staunton to keeping east of the South Fork of the Shenandoah for a spring on Waynesboro. Shields's renegade persona was no secret; he obviously felt that he could operate *carte blanche* in the Luray Valley, so McDowell was guilty of not restricting Shields's authority.

As for Brigadier General James Shields, his greatest fault in the whole affair was expressed in a letter he wrote to former Confederate general Richard Taylor in 1878—Shields was commending Taylor for his new book, *Destruction and Reconstruction*, and his description of the Battle of Port Republic. What Shields wrote as a statement of irony, really reads as an admission of culpability: "Now you will be surprised when I tell you that I have never been at Port Republic in my life."[79]

No one could fault James Shields if pangs of guilt struck him when he finished that sentence.

---

[79] Shields to Richard Taylor, March 21, 1878, Shields Papers.

"Worthy of a Higher Rank"
Colonel Joseph Thoburn and the Shenandoah Valley Campaigns

Scott C. Patchan

On October 24, 1864, the town of Wheeling, West Virginia, mourned the loss of Colonel Joseph Thoburn, a local hero who was gunned down five days earlier at the Battle of Cedar Creek. "The city was draped in mourning," reported the *Wheeling Daily Intelligencer.* "Flags at half-mast; emblems of mourning were hanging from the residences and places of business of our loyal people." Thousands of area residents flooded Mt. Wood Cemetery and the surrounding area to pay their last respects to Colonel Thoburn. "I seldom witnessed a more impressive ceremony," recalled Major General Samuel Heintzelman. "I was pleased to see the Presbyterians and Methodists fraternizing... There were many Copperheads to hear the loyal addresses." Yet for all of this outpouring of grief in 1864, Thoburn's name has been lost to all but the most dedicated students of the Civil War.[80]

Thoburn was born April 28, 1825, near Belfast, County Antrim in Northern Ireland. Later that year, his family immigrated to North America, ultimately settling on a farm near St. Clairsville, Ohio, not far from the Ohio River. On the opposite bank lay the northern panhandle of Virginia and the city of Wheeling, the area's central hub. In spite of limited educational opportunities, Thoburn attended medical school and became a doctor, eventually establishing a practice in Wheeling. Thoburn observed that the town was rapidly growing:

> *On every side it seems springing into life; new buildings on are every vacant spot springing up. Manufacturing and even commerce is being attracted here. And in a few weeks more we will have a direct rail road communication with the eastern cities and in another year a railroad*

---

[80] *Wheeling Daily Intelligencer,* October 25, 1864; Samuel Heintzelman Journal, Library of Congress, Washington, D.C.

connection the west. Great things are promised for us.
This is doubtless destined to be an important point.[81]

In spite of the booming local economy, Thoburn struggled with his fledgling medical practice, making ends meet with "a little pittance" from his mother.[82]

On December 13, 1853, he married Kate A. Mitchell, the daughter of a Methodist minister. The couple soon took six-year-old Gertrude Desal into their home. "Gerty" had come to America from Germany with her mother who was unable to care for her. Two years later, they added a child of their own, Anna Lyle, but difficulties soon followed. Unable to afford the cost of keeping his family in Wheeling due to his economically struggling medical practice, Thoburn's wife and daughter went to live with relatives in the country across the Ohio River.

Thoburn served many poor residents of the town and often understood that no payments would ever be forthcoming for his services, a constant drain on family finances. Over the course of twelve months, three of his patients died, prompting others to look elsewhere for medical care. One Wheeling lady quipped that the struggling Thoburn "could not be much of a physician or he would have a horse and buggy like other physicians." He accepted his economic woes in stride, not being overly concerned with "earthly" treasures. Through perseverance, his practice picked up, and he rented a house in town for his family. Then, tragedy struck when little Anna became sick and died in late September of 1857. Thoburn mourned: "The pattering of her little footsteps is no more heard upon the floor, but these old familiar sounds seem now to be echoing back from the deepest recesses of the heart. In imagination, I seem now to behold her playing 'bo peep' with me past the office door." Buoyed by faith, the Thoburns soldiered on. He reasoned, "The trial will do us good, and may not the education of heaven far exceed what we would or could give her here?"[83]

1858 brought renewed joy to the Thoburns; their first son, Matthew Martin was born in January. Two years later daughter Mary was born, and another girl arrived in 1862. His medical

---

[81] Joseph Thoburn Journal, Suzanne Pezick Private Collection, Greensboro, NC.
[82] Ibid.
[83] Ibid.

practice and financial situation continued to improve. His reputation for charity grew and people recognized that it "must have cost him no little personal sacrifice." It was said that Thoburn's charities "were almost as numerous as the days he lived and administered without pretension or ostentation."[84] One long-time acquaintance recalled Thoburn as:

> One of the most amiable of men, modest, humble and unassuming... His mind was vigorous and well informed on all general subjects, but especially in his medical profession. He was a skillful and tender physician and paid particular attention to the poor. His moral character was without a single stain.[85]

Although the Thoburns were living a happy and thriving life, sectional strife changed everything as it did for most Americans in 1861. When the Civil War broke out, Thoburn, like the majority of Wheeling residents, sided strongly with the Union.[86]

Long before the secession crisis fractured the nation, Thoburn prophetically opined that "the diabolical influence of slavery" would rip the United States asunder. When the war broke out in 1861, he enlisted as the regimental surgeon for the 1st Virginia (U.S.) Infantry. As a surgeon, he accompanied the regiment into the first organized land action of the war at the Battle of Philippi, Virginia, on June 3, 1861.[87] The resulting Union victory was critical in denying Confederates control of northwestern Virginia and allowed the region's Unionists to organize regiments and begin their march toward statehood. Among the few casualties at Philippi attended to by Thoburn was his commander, Colonel Benjamin F. Kelley.

After the Confederate victory at Manassas on July 21, 1861, it became clear that the war would be a long term affair. When the 1st Virginia reorganized for a three-year enlistment, Thoburn

---

[84] *Wheeling Daily Intelligencer,* July 18, 1865.

[85] Ibid., October 26, 1864.

[86] Ibid., October 24, 1864; J. H. Newton, G. G. Nichols and A. G. Sprankle, *History of the Pan-Handle: Being Historical Collections of the Counties of Ohio, Brooke, Marshall and Hancock, West Virginia.* (Wheeling, WV: L. A. Caldwell, 1879), 253.

[87] Philippi was fought in what is now West Virginia.

ascended from the regimental surgeon to the rank of colonel commanding the new organization. Thoburn's path carried him into the storied Shenandoah Valley, a locale that became the epicenter of his service. Thoburn experienced his first major battle on March 23, 1862, at Kernstown, a village three miles south of Winchester. There, Union forces attacked General Thomas J. "Stonewall" Jackson's small army who battled furiously from behind a sturdy stone wall. With Union forces unable to make any headway, Thoburn placed "his cap on the point of his sword and waving it to his men, called upon them to follow him in a dash across the open field and directly fronting the enemy's fire for the purpose of gaining a position on his flank." The gallant West Virginian led his men forward until a Southern bullet cut him down. Although severely wounded, Thoburn commanded his troops, "Go on and don't mind me, as I am not hurt," before struggling rearward in search of medical attention. His troops were unable to dislodge the Confederates, but Union reinforcements poured into the fight. Eventually, Union forces routed Jackson's army from the battlefield.[88]

A locomotive on the Baltimore and Ohio Railroad carried Thoburn home to Wheeling where he convalesced from his wound surrounded by his family. During the train ride home, Brigadier General Benjamin F. Kelley boarded the train and located Dr. Thoburn "in the mail car convenient to the water tank, nursing his arm as coolly as if it belonged to someone else." When he disembarked in Wheeling, the wounded hero quickly attracted a crowd. Observers noticed several bullet holes in his coat and pants as well as the one that shattered his arm "just a little." Well-wishers congratulated Thoburn, who "busied himself answering their desultory questions about the battle and the boys of the regiment."[89]

Colonel Erastus Tyler, Thoburn's brigade commander, wrote him congratulating him on "the soldierly and gallant conduct of yourself and command." He added, "Your conduct has won for you're [sic] a place among the bravest of the brave defenders of our country's cause." Tyler urged him to return to the Valley as soon as his recovery permitted, but it proved unnecessary, as Thoburn's

---

[88] Letter from One of Our 1st Virginia Boys," March 29, 1862, *Wheeling Daily Intelligencer*, April 4, 1862.
[89] "Colonel Joseph Thoburn," in ibid., March 29, 1862; Letter from One of Our 1st Virginia Boys," March 29, 1862, in ibid., April 4, 1862.

innate sense of duty did not allow him to linger in Wheeling. [90]

Although his wound had not fully healed, Thoburn returned to his command in late April. Shields's division marched up the muddy Luray Valley east of the Massanutten Mountain in hopes of blocking Jackson's line of retreat through the Blue Ridge, while Major General John C. Frémont's force pursued Jackson up the main Valley west of that mountain. But the cagey Jackson turned and defeated Frémont's force on June 8, defeating them at Cross Keys. The next day, Jackson turned east and attacked the vanguard of Shields's force at Port Republic. Tyler, Thoburn and the greatly outnumbered Union troops fought off several attacks before Jackson seized a vital Union artillery position on a hill known as "the Coaling." Then the Union line crumbled and retreated in confusion. A hatless Thoburn walked along behind the Union troops near the rear of the retreating mass, mistakenly believing that a rear guard stood between him and the Confederates. Suddenly, Southern cavalry charged and caught Thoburn by surprise. Jarred into action, he ordered the men to wheel and fire, dropping many Southerners from their saddles. An officer on a powerful iron-gray horse honed in on Thoburn and one of his captains, but the West Virginians fired their revolvers and shot him from his saddle. Jackson's victory at Port Republic marked the end of the 1862 Valley Campaign as "Stonewall" soon departed the Valley to join General Robert E. Lee in the defense of Richmond against General George B. McClellan and the Army of the Potomac. [91]

With Jackson's deceptive campaign in the Valley sapping manpower from the Union effort to capture Richmond, an overly-cautious McClellan did not press his advance. In late June, General Robert E. Lee turned and counterattacked, defeating McClellan in a serious of battles known as the Seven Days. However, even before McClellan's defeat, President Abraham Lincoln had grown weary of the cautious McClellan and created a new army in Virginia that Lincoln hoped would take a more aggressive approach to the war. Thoburn and the other forces from the Valley Campaign formed part of the newly created Army of Virginia under the command of

---

[90] Colonel E. B. Tyler to Colonel Joseph Thoburn, April 7, 1862, *Wheeling Daily Intelligencer*, April 15, 1862.
[91] Henry J. Johnson to Father, June 11, 1862, contained in ibid., June 23, 1862; James McElroy, "The Battle of Port Republic as I Saw It," copy of manuscript in author's possession.

Major General John Pope of Illinois.

Thoburn and the 1st West Virginia crossed to the east side of the Blue Ridge to join Pope. On August 9, they marched for Cedar Mountain south of Culpeper and arrived on the battlefield just as darkness ended the fighting. The campaign continued as a game of cat-and-mouse between the Union and Confederate forces between the Rappahannock and Rapidan Rivers. On August 17, Thoburn and his brigade commander, Colonel Samuel S. Carroll, conducted a reconnaissance along the Rapidan River. As they examined the enemy position on the opposite bank through field glasses, a Confederate sharpshooter fired and struck Carroll in the chest, ending his campaign and elevating Thoburn to brigade command. During this time, Thoburn became seriously ill, and only the "excitement of battle" kept him in the saddle and out of the hospital as Lee and Jackson defeated Pope at the Second Battle of Manassas. On August 30, a Confederate attack had forced the Union army to withdraw. Thoburn's brigade fell back from the front lines for nearly a mile and halted in an open field near Pittsylvania mansion north of the Warrenton Turnpike. Thoburn and his men thought they were in "perfect security" with another Union division posted between them and the enemy. His troops stacked arms and lounged about on the ground "talking about the fortunes of the day." Suddenly, a column of troops under Confederate general A. P. Hill emerged from a pine thicket across the dim field. In the darkness, Thoburn could not identity these troops but assumed they were friendly given his supposedly secure position. Uncertain, the ailing Thoburn ordered the brigade to arms and called out, "What troops are those?" A voice replied, "Secesh!" Still thinking that Union troops were supposed to be in his front, Thoburn shouted, "Don't talk that way or we'll give you a volley!" The voice yelled back, "Well, who are you?" Naively, Thoburn replied, "We are Union troops." A reply from across the field then called out, "Oh well then don't fire we're friends."[92]

These "friends" then advanced through the dark field in excellent order, prompting Thoburn to shout, "If you are Union troops, wave your colors." They complied, apparently having captured a U.S. battle flag, and marched to within "15 steps" of

---

[92] John V. Hadley to Miss Mollie J. Hill, September 16, 1862, *Indiana Magazine of History*, 59, no. 3 (1963): 189-288.

Thoburn's line, where they halted as if to stack arms. As Thoburn galloped over to them, one Confederate fired, barely missing the Colonel. He wheeled his horse around, and yelled to his men, "[It's] the enemy; fire!" An Indiana soldier in Thoburn's command reported: "At this instant a perfect sheet of flame proceeded from our ranks and from theirs. Simultaneous with the fire in front was another from our right flank, coming from a column that had slipped upon us unnoticed." Those troops threatened to surround Thoburn's brigade, and he ordered the men to "get out of there as best we could." The command evaded capture in the darkness, hurriedly making its way eastward across Bull Run and emerging in some disorder. As for Thoburn, the exigencies of battle and sickness had taxed him beyond the limits of human endurance. "He was perfectly prostrated when the battle was over," noted one of his men and was taken to the house of a senator in Alexandria, Virginia, where he lay "dangerously ill" and unable to return to duty until December.[93]

In January 1864, the commander of the Department of West Virginia Major General Benjamin F. Kelley eagerly recommended Thoburn for promotion to brigadier general. Kelley wrote, "Col. Thoburn I regard as an accomplished officer and in every way worthy of a higher rank." In spite of his experience and qualifications, Thoburn and the nascent state of West Virginia lacked the political clout needed to obtain the star worn by many lesser men with stronger political connections.[94]

In 1864 the ascension of Lieutenant General Ulysses S. Grant to supreme command of the Union army resulted in an all-out offensive across the South that returned Thoburn to the Shenandoah Valley under the command of the inept Major General Franz Sigel. In what had become the norm, Union arms suffered another defeat in the "Valley of humiliation" at New Market on May 15. Although defeated, the doctor from Wheeling took pride in his soldiers, who held the last line taking heavy casualties. He gushed, "No troops could have fought better but the enemy's line gradually

[93] John V. Hadley to Miss Mollie J. Hill, September 16, 1862, *Indiana Magazine,* 189-288; "Letter from Alexandria," September 3, 1862, *Wheeling Daily Intelligencer,* September 9, 1862,
[94] Correspondence of Benjamin F. Kelley to the U.S. War Department, January 1864, National Archives, Washington, D.C.; *Wheeling Daily Intelligencer,* February 22, 1864 and March 14, 1864.

enveloped our flanks and we had to give way." Of Sigel's impact on the battle, Thoburn wrote:

> *Our troops were posted in a very poor manner and were too much divided. A portion of the command had marched 20 miles before going into action and were not 10 minutes on the ground before they were engaged. Better positions were in the rear of what we occupied and if the troops in front had fallen back two miles we could have held our ground against more than opposed us. And had our force been brought into play together, the enemy would have been defeated.*[95]

Grant promptly relieved Sigel, replacing him with Major General David Hunter, a fiery abolitionist, who brought a harder brand of warfare to the Valley. Thoburn rejoiced at the change and observed, "Hunter will be a very poor Gen'l indeed if he is not better than Sigel." Hunter quickly whipped the army into shape and moved southward within a week's time. However, his policy of living off the land and burning homes where guerilla attacks occurred did not sit well with Thoburn. "I pity the poor inhabitants of the country through which we pass. Do the best we can, property will be destroyed and the innocent will suffer."[96]

Hunter's efforts achieved victory at the Battle of Piedmont on June 5, the bloodiest battle fought in the Valley to that date. With two failed attacks by the Union right wing and Confederates under Brigadier General William E. "Grumble" Jones prepping for a counterattack, Thoburn led a spirited attack into a gap in the rebel line that killed Jones and shattered the larger part of his force. The humble Thoburn attributed their success to "the favor of God" and the "gallant behavior" of his men, who captured 1,000 prisoners and three battle flags. Hunter's army occupied Staunton the next day and destroyed much of the Virginia Central Railroad in the Valley and the town's industrial capacity.[97]

Hunter received reinforcements from the mountains of West Virginia under General George Crook, and set-off to capture

---

[95] Thoburn Journal, typescript copy in possession of author.
[96] Ibid.
[97] Ibid.

Lynchburg, Virginia, a vital railroad and logistical center east of the Blue Ridge. If Hunter could capture Lynchburg, Lee and the Army of Northern Virginia would find themselves experiencing major logistical problems that could threaten their ability to hold Richmond. Hunter continued up the Valley, stopping at Lexington to burn the Virginia Military Institute, whose cadets had taken part in the Battle of New Market. He also burned the home of former Virginia governor John Letcher. While Thoburn continued to lament the suffering of civilians, he noted those burnings without comment.

Hunter's army crossed the Blue Ridge at the Peaks of Otter and arrived in front of Lynchburg late on June 17. Although his advance drove the Confederate cavalry from the town's outer defenses, the vanguard of the Army of Northern Virginia's Second Corps arrived that evening, ending the opportunity Hunter had to capture the vital railroad town. Some indecisive see-saw combat occurred the following day, but Hunter decided to retreat westward through the Roanoke Valley into the Mountains of West Virginia at the suggestion of George Crook. Although they evaded General Jubal A. Early by this route, the scarcity of food in the sparsely populated mountains wore heavily on the troops. As they struggled across Big Sewell Mountain in late June, Thoburn observed: "The road is lined for miles with broken down and starving men who are sent forward in advance of the main body. The horses are staggering and falling down from exhaustion." As they neared Charleston, Thoburn wrote: "One month's time will not restore the vigor of health that was enjoyed before the raid began. To restore good discipline will require equally as long a time and to make good the evil we have done is simply impossible."[98] Thoburn remained outspoken about the retreat and conduct of the army during the raid, and earned the ire of Hunter in the process.

While Hunter retreated through West Virginia to the Ohio River, Jubal Early marched his army of 16,000 troops north of the Potomac River. He won a victory at Monocacy Junction on July 9, and arrived at the gates of Washington on July 11, before withdrawing toward Virginia on July 12, when faced with large Union reinforcements reaching Washington. Thoburn and the vanguard of Hunter's army returned to active operations in tracking

---

[98] Thoburn Journal, typescript copy in possession of author.

Early down at the battle of Snickers Gap or Cool Spring on July 18. George Crook sent Thoburn, now in command of a full division, on a flank march up the Shenandoah River to get around what Crook believed was only a strong rear guard at the main crossing. Thoburn's command forded the river and began to deploy on the west bank. Contrary to Crook's assumption, Early's entire army remained in the area and two divisions turned on Thoburn. Major General Robert Rodes's veteran Confederate division crashed in on the West Virginian's right flank, sending most of his men retreating in confusion across the Shenandoah River. Although reinforcements were arriving on the opposite bank, the confusing scene convinced their commander, Major General James B. Ricketts, to forgo crossing the river and joining Thoburn.

The situation bordered on catastrophic for Thoburn's command, with one West Virginian describing it as "a Bull Run panic." Thoburn, the only man on horseback, braved the bullets directed at him and fashioned a last ditch battle line in a sunken road behind a stone wall. One Union soldier recalled, "many brave men fell into the second line and remained, but as an organization, the rest fled and did not come back." Swarmed over by the fugitives, Thoburn's second line began to waver. If it did not hold, "it would be Ball's Bluff reenacted." Thoburn, "the coolest man on the field," steadied the troops by his example and deftly shifted the 116th Ohio from his left to the beleaguered right flank, securing that critical sector of his battle line.[99]

Rodes attacked Thoburn three more times. Although Thoburn lacked the troops to fully cover his position, Rodes did not launch an overwhelming coordinated attack nor did a second nearby Confederate division join the offensive. This permitted Thoburn to shift troops to the threatened sector. "He exposed himself wherever the fire was heaviest," recalled a soldier of the 12th West Virginia, "and there commanded in person, being all the time mounted and therefore a mark, it is strange he was not struck." While Thoburn came out unscathed, both his adjutant and orderly were wounded in the combat. At Cool Spring, Thoburn conducted combat operations as an independent commander quickly reacting to the situation and saving his command from disaster. Although victory belonged to the Confederates, he and the men who

---

[99] *Wheeling Daily Intelligencer*, July 25, 1864.

remained on the west bank had achieved a sort of moral victory holding out with their backs to the river in the face of overwhelming odds. All in all, he had done well in his first effort as a division commander under the circumstances.[100] Six days later, Thoburn took part in the Second Battle of Kernstown on July 24. Crook again misread Early's deployments and his army was routed and driven back into Maryland. Thoburn's division covered the retreat, and he became lost in the darkness and was cut-off from the army. He escaped by heading out on foot to the west through the Alleghany Mountains until he made his way to the Baltimore and Ohio Railroad. Crook's defeat opened the door for Early to burn Chambersburg, Pennsylvania, in retaliation for Hunter's destruction of the homes of several prominent Confederates near Shepherdstown and Charlestown.

In early August, Grant assigned command of the Shenandoah Valley to Major General Philip H. Sheridan and gave him an army that ultimately numbered nearly 40,000 men in the field. Thoburn continued as a division commander, fighting in several small engagements throughout August and September. On September 19, Sheridan won a resounding and unprecedented victory at the Third Battle of Winchester, or Opequon Creek as the Union called it, and although Thoburn began the day in reserve, he ended up playing a decisive role in that battle. With the tide of battle ebbing and flowing and neither side able to hold the advantage, Sheridan ordered Crook to reinforce the hard-hit Nineteenth Army Corps on the right flank. Crook examined the situation and determined to take one of his divisions on a flank march to the north, leaving Thoburn to relieve the Nineteenth Corps in a woodlot known as the First Woods.

Sheridan found Thoburn moving into those woods and ordered him to attack when he heard Duval's troops advancing on his right flank. Sheridan spoke in the "the most enthusiastic terms" to impress upon Thoburn the importance of his advance through an open field toward the Confederates who waited on the other side sheltered in the Second Woods and ravines. General Sheridan then waved and shouted to Thoburn's troops, yelling, "Go for 'em boys!"

---

[100] *Wheeling Daily Intelligencer*, July 25, 1864; Thomas F. Wildes, *Record of the One Hundred and Sixteenth Regiment, Ohio Infantry Volunteers in the War of the Rebellion* (Sandusky, OH: I.F. Mack & Bros., Printers, 1884), 130-131.

The men responded with enthusiastic cheers for the army commander.[101]

Before long, Thoburn's command heard cheers "as only the Army of West Virginia knows how to cheer," signaling the appearance of Crook's flanking on the right north of Red Bud Run. Thoburn's division advanced in a double line of battle and charged across the field toward the Confederate division of Major General John B. Gordon that unleashed a torrent of lead at the Union troops.[102] An onlooker from the Nineteenth Corps observed Thoburn's advance:

> The broad blue wave surged forward with a yell which lasted for minutes. In response there arose from the northern front of the woods a continuous, deafening wail of musketry without break or tremor. For a time I despaired of the success of the attack, for it did not seem possible that any troops could endure such a fire.[103]

As Thoburn advanced, the Confederates began firing into his left flank, but "The instincts of the soldier prompted the proper movement before my commands could be conveyed," reported Thoburn. "Each man was marching and facing toward the enemy's fire."[104] The attack drove the Confederates from the woods, but they soon rallied behind stone walls and earthen fortifications, temporarily forcing Thoburn's men to halt and take cover. It did not last long. Sheridan attacked with the Sixth Corps to the south while the Union cavalry thundered up the Valley Pike flanking the Confederates out of every position they attempted to hold. Sheridan sent Jubal Early and his army "Whirling through Winchester," in a victory that forever changed the balance of power in the Shenandoah Valley. Thoburn's journal for this period has not been located. However, given the defeats he had endured in the Union's "Valley of humiliation," he no doubt relished the moment, thanked

---

[101] A West Virginia Officer to Editors *Intelligencer*, October 10, 1864, *Wheeling Daily Intelligencer*. October 19, 1864; Henry A. DuPont, *The Campaign of 1864 in the Valley of Virginia and the Expedition to Lynchburg* (New York: National Americana Society, 1925), 120-21.

[102] *Wheeling Daily Intelligencer*, October 19, 1864.

[103] John W. DeForest, *A Volunteers Adventure: A Union Captain's Record of the Civil War* (New Haven: Yale University Press, 1946), 186-188.

[104] *OR* ser. I, vol. 43, pt. I, 368-369.

God for his blessings, and prayed for a quick end to the war so he could soon be home with his family in Wheeling.[105]

Sheridan pursued Early the very next day and caught up with him at Fisher's Hill, a strong position just south of Strasburg that was known as the Gibraltar of the Valley. Crook called Thoburn and his fellow division commander Colonel Rutherford B. Hayes to Sheridan's headquarters. Together they convinced Sheridan to allow Crook to conduct a flank march on the eastern face of Little North Mountain to drive Early from his position. The attack worked as Thoburn's division rolled up the Confederate breastworks and Hayes's command plowed through the Confederate rear. They charged for three miles, yelling and firing, and did not stop until they reached the Valley Pike. The Sixth and Nineteenth Corps joined in the attack, and Sheridan's army won its second decisive victory in three days, capturing 1,000 prisoners and as many as twenty cannon.

The victory might have ended the campaign, but Sheridan's cavalry failed to break through from the Luray Valley and cut-off Early's retreat. Instead, Early regrouped in Brown's Gap where reinforcements from the Army of Northern Virginia arrived with a directive from Lee to make things right for the Confederacy again in the Shenandoah Valley. Nevertheless, Sheridan felt that the campaign was over and withdrew down the Valley, burning the farms and driving off the livestock from one end of the Valley to the other so that Early could no longer subsist on the abundance of the region's agriculture. Given Thoburn's reservations about similar but very limited actions by Hunter, he surely grieved for the suffering civilians in the wake of the organized and widespread destruction wrought by "the Burning."

Although the federals thought the campaign was over, Jubal Early cautiously followed them down the Valley. Sheridan's confident army went into camp along the banks of Cedar Creek a few miles north of Strasburg while Early lingered at Fisher's Hill. At 5:30 on the morning of October 19, the Confederates launched a devastating surprise attack on the Union army. Caught completely off-guard with most soldiers still asleep in their tents, Thoburn's division was thoroughly routed, never regaining full cohesion for most of the daylong Battle of Cedar Creek. Thoburn rode toward

---

[105] *OR* ser. I, vol. 43, pt. 2, 114-115, 123-124.

Middletown, then paused briefly and peered back at the Confederates through his field glasses. Reaching the town, he worked feverishly to disentangle his wagon train and get it moving toward Winchester. Bedlam ruled the scene as Colonel William Payne's Confederate cavalry charged toward the trains in the town. A mounted trooper in a Union uniform rode up to Thoburn and ordered him to halt. Engrossed in his efforts to save the wagons, Thoburn ignored him, "not knowing the Rebel was a foe and not knowing that it was himself addressed." The blue-coated Confederate shot Thoburn in the chest, knocking him from his horse in a vacant lot. After lying there for ten minutes, Mrs. Mary Hoover of Middletown came to his aid. With the assistance of a kind Confederate, they turned him over to make him more comfortable. Thoburn asked Mary to hold his hand and implored her to write to his wife, Kate. He asked that Mary tell Kate that his only "regret was to leave his wife and children. O, he said, how I would love to see them here. He said he was prepared for death, prepared to meet his God. He told me to give you a dying farewell, and for you all to meet him in heaven where there would be no more parting." Mary lingered until artillery shells rained down on the area, sending her to seek shelter.

When a lull in the battle occurred, Thoburn was taken into a nearby home. Sheridan counterattacked, recovered the lost ground and delivered another crushing defeat on Early. When Thoburn's comrades located him later that evening, they summoned surgeons to examine the wound. One declared the wound mortal, saying he would not live through the night. Thoburn, himself a doctor, calmly replied that "the news did not shock him in the least that he had known after the first ten minutes his wound was mortal and he was ready to meet his fate." He died at 12:02 A.M. on October 20.[106] His death elicited expressions of grief throughout the army of West Virginia. "We are all sorry that he was killed," lamented a Connecticut foot soldier; "He was one of the best officers in our corps."[107]

The greatest loss was felt by his family back in Wheeling. The husband and father was irreplaceable. For Kate Thoburn, the

---

[106] Mary Hoover did indeed write to Mrs. Thoburn. *Wheeling Daily Intelligencer,* October 24 and 26, 1864.

[107] Charles Lynch, *The Civil War Diary of Charles H. Lynch, 18th Connecticut Volunteers.* (Hartford, CT: The Case, Lockwood, and Brainard Co., 1915), 130.

grief of losing her husband and rearing their children alone remained a lifelong burden. On December 13, 1864, the anniversary of their wedding, she added this entry in the back of his journal:

Eleven years ago this day, I was married to the writer of this book. A nobler and braver man never lived. On the 19th of October, he sacrificed his life to his country. With three little children of our love, I am left to mourn my great and irreparable loss. My heart is torn, and I feel that all is gone. He was my idol, my strong support. On him I rested. O' what shall I do now. How great my responsibility. Where will I be when eleven more years pass 'round. Perhaps I with my beloved. May God grant that when death comes to me I may join him and may our family be unbroken.[108]

---

[108] Katherine Thoburn, contained in Colonel Thoburn's Journal, Suzanne Pezick Private Collection, Greensboro, NC.

After the Civil War in the Shenandoah Valley:
Excerpts from the Freedmen's Bureau Papers

Jonathan A. Noyalas

Less than one year after the Civil War's end Watkins James, a resident of Winchester who served as assistant United States assessor, offered testimony to members of Congress who served on the Joint Committee on Reconstruction. When Michigan senator Jacob Howard asked James his "opinion" on the "feeling[s] of the once rebel people towards the government of the United States" James replied: "I have come to the conclusion, from travelling through the country, that their feelings toward the government, towards Union men, and towards the freedmen, are more hostile to-day than they were at the close of the rebellion."[109]

In an effort to ameliorate conditions for African Americans in that "hostile" environment—one that existed not just in the Shenandoah Valley but throughout all of the former Confederacy—the Federal government turned to agents of the Bureau of Refugees, Freedmen, and Abandoned Lands (Freedmen's Bureau). Established in March 1865 the Freedmen's Bureau assumed various responsibilities in the Civil War's aftermath— reunite families busted apart by slavery, assist African Americans in finding employment, support education of African Americans, provide medical care to newly freed-people, ensure even-handed application of law by civil authorities, and promote long-term economic stability.[110]

Nearly two months after its establishment President Andrew Johnson appointed General Oliver O. Howard as its chief.[111] Within

---

[109] Testimony of Watkins James, February 2, 1866, in *Report of the Joint Committee on Reconstruction at the First Session Thirty-Ninth Congress, Part II Virginia, North Carolina, South Carolina* (Washington, D.C.: Government Printing Office, 1866), 39-40.

[110] For an overview of the Freedmen's Bureau's many functions see Paul A. Cimbala, *The Freedmen's Bureau: Reconstructing the American South after the Civil War* (Malabar, FL: Krieger, 2005).

[111] Jeffrey R. Kerr-Ritchie, *Freedpeople in the Tobacco South: Virginia, 1860-1900* (Chapel Hill: University of North Carolina Press, 1999), 34.

weeks after assuming the awesome responsibilities of the Freedmen's Bureau, Howard appointed nine assistant commissioners. Among Howard's nine choices was Colonel Orlando Brown. The Connecticut native assumed his mantle as assistant commissioner on May 31, 1865, and began the task of establishing the Freedmen's Bureau throughout Virginia. From his headquarters in Richmond, Brown divided Virginia into ten districts and appointed assistant commissioners.[112]

In Virginia's Shenandoah Valley the Freedmen's Bureau had offices located in Winchester, Front Royal, Woodstock, Harrisonburg, Staunton, and Lexington. Initially, the Freedmen's Bureau in the Shenandoah Valley was part of Virginia's Sixth District, but reorganizations after September 1866 made it part of the Commonwealth's Ninth District.[113]

During its seven years of existence in Virginia the agents of the Freedmen's Bureau produced massive amounts of documentary evidence, which now occupy 203 rolls of microfilm at the National Archives and Records Administration in Washington, D.C. Although these records offer one of the most compelling windows into life in the Shenandoah Valley in the war's immediate aftermath and offer enormous insight into the manner in which the region's African Americans attempted to integrate into a society that regarded them as social and political unequals, it has been a grossly underutilized source.

Although some portions of the Freedmen's Bureau records pertinent to the Shenandoah Valley's postwar story have been digitized as part of Edward L. Ayers groundbreaking "Valley of the Shadow Project," it does not provide a complete transcription of thousands of pages of Shenandoah Valley Freedmen's Bureau records contained on twenty-one rolls of microfilm.

This annotated portion of Freedmen's Bureau Records is derived from three of those twenty-one rolls (89, 183, and 187). These excerpts, while largely focused on the lower Shenandoah Valley, do

---

[112] Richard Lowe, *Republicans and Reconstruction in Virginia, 1856-70* (Charlottesville: University Press of Virginia, 1991), 29. Reginald Washington et. al., *Records of the Field Offices for the State of Virginia, Bureau of Refugees, Freedmen and Abandoned Lands, 1865-1872* (Washington, D.C.; National Archives and Records Administration, 2006), 3. Virginia was divided into ten districts until April 14, 1867. On April 15, 1867, the ten districts were reorganized into ten subdistricts.
[113] Washington, et. al. *Records of the Field Offices*, 16-17.

on occasion offer important glimpses into postwar life in other parts of the Shenandoah Valley, namely Harrisonburg and Lexington. Although the records of the Freedmen's Bureau are mostly concerned with issues related to ameliorating the condition for African Americans in the region, they also provide valuable insight into the lengths to which some former Confederates in the region would go in order to show their disdain for the Federal government or Union soldiers who occupied the area. Additionally, this particular group of excerpted records provides a glimpse into the manners in which those who supported the Confederacy continued to show reverence for the Confederate cause after the Civil War's guns fell silent in the spring of 1865.

Uncertainty as to How to Assist Former Slaves

In the war's aftermath federal troops posted in the Shenandoah Valley looked for guidance on how to support and aid the region's African Americans as they searched for a way to realize "freedom." The following excerpts reveal the concerns Union officers possessed about how best to help former slaves.

General Isaac Duval[114] to General Alfred T.A. Torbert[115]
June 9, 1865
Staunton, Virginia.

The condition of the Negro families in this vicinity is in my

---

[114] Isaac Hardin Duval was born September 1, 1824, in Wellsburg, Virginia (later West Virginia). Prior to the Civil War he spent time as a hunter and trapper in the American West. At the outset of the Civil War he became major of the 1st Virginia (U.S.) Infantry. During General Philip H. Sheridan's 1864 Shenandoah Campaign he commanded a division in General George Crook's Eighth Corps (Army of West Virginia). He was wounded at the Third Battle of Winchester on September 19, 1864, and promoted to brigadier general on September 24, 1864. After his military service he held a number of political posts including member of the House of Representatives between 1869-1871 representing the state of West Virginia. He died in July 1902. For additional information see Ezra J. Warner, *Generals in Blue: Lives of the Union Commanders* (Baton Rouge: Louisiana State University Press, 1992), 134.
[115] General Alfred Thomas Archimedes Torbert, a native of Delaware, graduated from West Point in 1855. During the 1864 Shenandoah Campaign Torbert commanded General Philip H. Sheridan's cavalry. He resigned from military service on October 31, 1866. He was killed on August 29, 1880, when the *Vera Cruz* wrecked off the coast of Cape Canaveral. For additional information see ibid., 508-09.

opinion becoming alarming. Large families of women and small children are being driven from their homes daily and hundreds of them are now roaming over the country begging for their support.

Upon investigation I find that in nearly every instance the Fathers of the families now being turned out have gone North with the U.S. army during the war, and as their farmer masters now claim that they have not the means to support them, they are turned destitute, and almost naked to beg for their food.

I deem this a matter of vast importance to the community at large and earnestly recommend immediate action in order that I may know what dispositions to make application to me for relief.[116]

J.H. McKenzie to Captain Wm. Stover How[117]
August 1, 1865
Winchester, Virginia

I would like instructions in regard to the settlement of questions of dispute between colored and colored and colored and whites. I have no instructions on the subject and have had several cases referred to me already. One case was referred to me this morning by General Torbert, a white man complains that he hired three colored men to work for him until Christmas and that they ran away from him, stealing from him $80 in gold, 300 lb. bacon and several other articles. I have sent for the parties to investigate the matter and expressed the opinion to the Provost Marshall that such cases should be tried by the military court. I would like information on the subject.

There are a great may colored children in this town and I think that a school should be established here.

I am likely to have a great deal of trouble with the freedmen they are very shiftless and do not stick to their contracts, what should be done with a freedmen who makes a contract and violates it immediately

---

[116] Letter of General Isaac Duval to General Alfred T.A. Torbert, June 9, 1865. Roll 187 Unregistered Letters Received, June 1865-December 1868, Records of the Field Offices for the State of Virginia, Bureau of Refugees, Freedmen, and Abandoned Lands, 1865-1872, National Archives and Records Administration, Washington, D.C. Hereafter cited as BRF&AL.

[117] Captain William Stover How served as the superintendent of the sixth district from August 1865-May 1866.

afterwards and goes to work for another party. He is not a vagrant because he is at work. Yet he has broken in contract.[118]

Displays of Confederate Sentiment After the War

Although the Federal government implemented measures to limit the public display of Confederate symbols in the conflict's immediate aftermath, former Confederates attempted to show devotion to the Confederate cause in a variety of ways. The following excerpts reveal the methods employed by some at various locations in the Shenandoah Valley to display pro-Confederate sympathies after the conflict.[119]

Lieutenant J.H. Hall[120] to Magistrates of Woodstock, Virginia
July 21, 1866

Sirs,

I must request that these proceedings to which we are subject, such as singing at all hours of the night, the discharge of fire arms, ringing of bells, cheers for prominent rebels &c, be immediately stopped as they are not only disloyal, but emphatically nuisances, and their originators disturbers of the peace. Please inform me without delay what action can and will be taken in this matter.[121]

Two days after Hall submitted his note to authorities in Woodstock, officials from Woodstock replied to Lieutenant Hall.

---

[118] Letter of J.H. McKenzie to Captain W. Stover How, August 1, 1865, Roll 187 Unregistered Letters Received, June 1865-December 1868, BRF&AL.

[119] For additional discussions of this see Jonathan A. Noyalas, *Civil War Legacy in the Shenandoah: Remembrance, Reunion, and Reconciliation* (Charleston, SC: The History Press, 2015), 17-28. For discussions beyond the Shenandoah Valley see William Blair, *Cities of the Dead: Contesting the Memory of the Civil War in the South: 1861-1914* (Chapel Hill: University of North Carolina Press, 2004), 50.

[120] Records indicate that Lieutenant J.H. Hall served as adjutant of the 1st United States Cavalry from September 7, 1866-November 7, 1869. For additional information on Hall see Francis B. Heitman, *Historical Register and Dictionary of the United States Army, From Its Organization, September 29, 1798 to March 2, 1903* (Washington, D.C.: Government Printing Office, 1903), 1: 66.

[121] Letter of Lieutenant J.H. Hall to Magistrates of Woodstock, Virginia, Roll 187 Unregistered Letters Received, June 1865-December 1868, BRF&AL.

Letter of Woodstock Officials to Lieutenant J.H. Hall
July 23, 1866

Dear Sir,

Your circular to the magistrates of Woodstock of the 21st inst. requesting the suppression of rebel demonstrations in honor of rebel victories and rebel chieftans &c &c is received.

In reply I have to say that while those demonstrations are very annoying and insulting to loyal men, to those of us who followed the flag of the Union during the late rebellion; yet I know of no law of Virginia under which we as civil magistrates could take action... and until better informed, those traitors will be able to exult in their same, until there is an open outbreak or retribution meets them in some other way. Let them "slide"... in the future they may be possessed of... reason and more patriotic feelings.[122]

Report of Lieutenant George Cook[123] from Harrisonburg, Virginia
May 5, 1866

Reports that some boys aged 14 and under paraded the streets with a Confederate flag and hollered and yelled in passing.[124]

Report of Lieutenant. J.H. Hall from Woodstock, Virginia
August 16, 1866

Lt. Hall asst. supt. at Woodstock, Va. reports that ten men dressed in Rebel uniforms have used insulting language towards him and his officers. Requests the arrest of the parties... a civil magistrate having refused [to] arrest them.[125]

---

[122] Letter of Woodstock official George [illegible] to Lieutenant J.H. Hall, July 23, 1866, Roll 187 Unregistered Letters Received, June 1865-December 1868, BRF&AL.

[123] George Cook served as lieutenant of the 109th United States Colored Troops during the Civil War. For additional details on his service see Heitman, *Historical Register*, 1: 323.

[124] Report of Lieutenant George Cook, May 5, 1866, Roll 183 Endorsements Sent, November 1865-June 1866, BRF&AL.

[125] Report of Lieutenant J.H. Hall, August 14, 1866, in ibid.

Violence Against African Americans and Union Troops

In the Civil War's aftermath some former Confederates could not accept defeat and certainly refused to accept African Americans as equals. While examples exist of former Confederates violently lashing out at Union soldiers stationed in the Shenandoah Valley, they were not the only targets of violence and intimidation. In addition to African Americans in the Shenandoah Valley, those who worked as teachers in the Freedmen's Schools throughout the region also confronted frequent and severe threats.[126]

Statement of Franklin Lambert to Lieutenant James H. Hall
February 19, 1866

Personally appeared before me this 19th day of Feby. 1866. Franklin Lambert who made the following sworn statement.

That on or about the 6th day of Feby. 1866 when near Columbia Furnace on the Woodstock Road where in pursuit beneath thick bush I felt the wind of a bullet pass my face & I heard the report of a gun. I started back immediately after another ball passed through the valise I had in my hand.

I was informed by two parties, before I was fired upon, that I had better leave this part of the country.[127]

Statement of G.H. Harrison to Lieutenant J.H. Hall
February 27, 1866

A statement of G.H. Harrison teacher of freedmen's school at Massanutten that he was taken out by 10 or 15 men, armed and disguised at 9 or 10 p.m. and immersed twice in the Shenandoah River, and his life threatened unless he left in three days.

Lt. Hall states that his force is too small to arrest the parties in

---

[126] For general discussions of the violence confronted by teachers in the Civil War's aftermath see Ronald E. Butchart, *Schooling the Freed People: Teaching, Learning, and the Struggle for Black Freedom, 1861-1876* (Chapel Hill: University of North Carolina Press, 2010), 153-178. For additional experiences of teachers in the Shenandoah Valley see Wayne E. Reilly, ed., *Sarah Jane Foster Teacher of the Freedmen: A Diary and Letters* (Charlottesville: University Press of Virginia, 1990).

[127] Statement of Franklin Lambert to Lieutenant J.H. Hall, February 19, 1866, Roll 187 Unregistered Letters Received, June 1865-December 1868, BRF&AL.

present state of public feeling—requests that a squad of cavalry be sent.

Lt. Hall did not believe, that without additional military support, the Freedmen's Bureau would continue to function properly. He explained on February 13, 1866.

If proper means are not taken to check these rebellious outlaws, the freedmen's schools must be abandoned and the authority of this District be rendered contemptible by the absence of all power to protect officers, agents, and the freedmen from outrage and murder.[128]

Once Lieutenant Hall informed his superiors about the violent attacks against Mr. Harrison, General Winfield Scott Hancock the commander of the Middle Military Division, of which the Shenandoah Valley was part, established a special commission "for trial of the perpetrators of the outrage upon the teacher Mr. Harrison."[129]

Statement of Assault in Lexington, Virginia
June 14, 1866

Reports that a colored boy was assaulted by the son of his employer named Brockenbrough, that the boy after being assaulted... the magistrate decided that the boy having left Brockenbrough's service, without notice was not entitled to the pay then due, although Brockenbrough admitted that until the assault the boy had always worked faithfully.[130]

That this son of Brockenbrough was the same who assaulted a little negro for singing patriotic songs in the street.[131]

---

[128] Statement of G.H. Harrison to Lieutenant J.H. Hall, Woodstock, February 27, 1866. Roll 183 Endorsements Sent, November 1865-June 1866, BRF&AL.

[129] Military commission established in Harrison Case, March 31, 1866, in ibid.

[130] Referring to Judge John W. Brockenbrough. In 1845 he was appointed by President James K. Polk as judge for the United States Court for the Western District of Virginia. He held that post until 1861. For additional biographical information see Ezra J. Warner and W. Buck Yearns, *Biographical Register of the Confederate Congress* (Baton Rouge: Louisiana State University Press, 1975), 33.

[131] Statement of assault against "a colored boy" in Lexington, Virginia, June 14, 1866, Roll 183 Endorsements Sent, November 1865-June 1866, BRF&AL.

Report of Attempted Rape by
Cadet from the Virginia Military Institute
June 14, 1866

Reports that a cadet named Tuntsell attempted to commit a rape on a colored girl in the Lexington Hotel.[132] That we advised the girl's father for a warrant to arrest Tuntsell, but that the colored man has been advised by some of the provincial citizens not to do so.[133]

Report of Captain Gilbert R. Chandler[134]
Assistant Superintendent
October 9, 1866
Winchester, VA

Letter (dated Washington Oct 1ˢᵗ 66) states that a teacher was locked in a school house near Winchester Va which was burned with him fastened in and that at Buckton the col'd people are prevented from attending divine worship by the insults and abuse of the secessionists.[135]

Report of Captain E.H. Ripley to Jno. McDonnell
January 13, 1868

I have the honor to submit the following statement in the case of James Lucas (col'd.) and William Castleman (white) both of Berryville Clark[e] Co. Va. On the 1ˢᵗ day of Jan. Lucas wen to Castleman's kitchen

---

[132] There are no cadets listed as attending the Virginia Military Institute at this time with the surname "Tuntsell." There are, however, three cadets with the name Tunstall who attended at the time, all members of the class of 1867—James Levi Tunstall, John Liggat Tunstall, and Richard Baylor Tunstall. See Historical Rosters Database, Virginia Military Institute, Class of 1867, Accessed September 15, 2017.
http://archivesweb.vmi.edu/rosters/index.php?VMIClass=1867

[133] Report of Rape by Cadet Tuntsell at Lexington Hotel, June 14, 1866, in Roll 183 Endorsements Sent, November 1865-June 1866, BRF&AL.

[134] Chandler served as a captain in the 16ᵗʰ Michigan Infantry during the Civil War and lost an arm during the conflict. He then served as an officer in the 19ᵗʰ Veteran Reserve Corps. Michigan congressman John F. Driggs praised Chandler in a letter to General Ulysses S. Grant on August 24, 1867, and believed "Chandler, a brave and accomplished one armed soldier." For additional information see John Y. Simon, ed., *The Papers of Ulysses S. Grant: January 1-September 30, 1867* (Carbondale: Southern Illinois University Press, 1991), 17: 383; Gilbert R. Chandler, 19ᵗʰ Veteran Reserve Corps, Compiled Military Service Record, RG 94, Indexes to the Carded Records of Soldiers Who Served in Volunteer Organizations during the Civil War, National Archives and Records Administration, Washington, D.C.

[135] Report of Captain Gilbert Chandler, October 9, 1866, Roll 183 Endorsements Sent, November 1865-June 1866, BRF&AL.

cursed and otherwise abused his customer's servants. He was [word illegible] of that part of the house by Mrs. Castleman. He did not go out, used very harsh language to Mrs. C—then Mr. C—was called and he ordered him out of the house then Lucas curses him and used force against Mr. C—then Castleman beat him with his walking stick first in the public sitting room with his cane. After Lucas went in the street he said that he would kill Castleman, then C—went out and beat him in the street and... struck him six times with his walking stick.

Lucas went to Mr. Pullen [?] a magistrate for a warrant to make Castleman pay for beating him. Pullen [?] told Lucas that he could not issue any such warrant, but if he Lucas wanted a warrant to make Castleman keep the peace he would give him one, if he Lucas wanted damages he must appeal to a lawyer. Lucas left saying he would have a warrant to make Castleman pay him.

Lucas acknowledged to me and to Mr. Pullen [?] that he was drunker than he had been for 12 (twelve) years and he did not want anything... I think Lucas was under the influence of liquor... The magistrate will issue a warrant to make Castleman keep the peace.[136]

Summoned to Solve All Problems

In the Civil War's aftermath former slaves viewed the Freedmen's Bureau as an institution that would not only provide support in integrating into a society that regarded them as unequal, but as the ultimate arbiter of all things including property disputes and domestic issues.

Extracted report of Captain Gilbert R. Chandler
Asst. Supt.
January 3, 1867
Winchester, Virginia

States (Jany3/67) that Charity Wilson, a freedwoman has complained that her husband Jackson Wilson has deserted her and is now living with a woman named Ann Wilson... she requests the arrest and

---

[136] Report of Captain E.H. Ripley to Jno. McDonnell, January 13, 1868, Roll 89, Letters Sent, May 1866-December 1868, BRF&AL.

punishment of Jackson Wilson.[137]

Bureau R. F & A Land Head Qrs. 9th Dist. Va
Winchester, Virginia April 6, 1867

Respectfully referred to Maj. Genl. Schofield...[138] *The property in this referred to as will be seen by the enclosed and belonging in 1861 as it does at this time to the Gen. Conference of the Ministers and Preachers of the Methodist Episcopal Church. During the war a portion of this conference with the state seceded and established what is now called the Episcopal Methodist Church and took possession of the church property in Winchester and Berryville. After the war closed, Gen. Ayres, commanding this district issued an order restoring the property to its original owners and the within named church was taken possession of by the representatives of the Genl. Conference. Shortly afterwards permission was given by the Rev. McMullen (the representative of the Genl. Conference) to the Episcopal Methodists to hold service in the church on alternate Sabbaths, but as soon as the latter obtained the key, the door was locked against the ministers and members of the Genl. Conference some of whom were arrested for endearing [?] to gain admittance and bound over to keep the peace. Subsequently application was made to Judge Parker for an injunction on the property by the ministers of the Genl. Conference of the M.E. Church which was refused on the ground that the Genl. Conference were aliens and foreigners. The opinion of Mr. Conrad, a prominent Rebel and Lawyer is herewith transmitted.*

Application was made to Maj. Brown comd. officer of this post for restoration of the property in Sept. last, but as no action appears to have been taken on the premises, and as no copy of the deed has been filed, Rev. McMullen renews the application.[139]

---

[137] Extracted report of Captain Gilbert R. Chandler, January 3, 1867, Roll 183 Endorsements Sent, November 1865-June 1866, BRF&AL.

[138] Schofield took command of the Department of the Potomac, of which Virginia was part, in August 1866. Not in favor of universal suffrage for African Americans Schofield held his post in Virginia until June 1, 1868, when he assumed the role of secretary of war in President Andrew Johnson's administration. For additional reading about Schofield and Reconstruction in Virginia see James L. McDonough, "John Schofield as Military Director of Reconstruction in Virginia" *Civil War History* 15, no. 3 (1969): 237-256.

[139] Statement on Church Ownership in Berryville and Winchester, Virginia, April 6, 1867, Roll 183, Endorsements Sent, November 1865-June 1866, BRF&AL.

Letter of Captain E.H. Ripley to James Boyd Esq.
Bur. R.F. & A. Lands
Office Warren Co. Front Royal, Virginia
May 11, 1866

You are hereby notified that Bushrod Johnson (colored) has applied to me to collect wages for his wife Mahaler [sp.?] Johnson (colored) for services rendered you.

I respectfully request you will call on this office this day or as soon as thereupon as possible & settle said claim.[140]

Report of Captain E.H. Ripley on Cases of Abuses and Fraud
April 30, 1868

During the past month there have been several cases of abuse and fraud practiced upon the freedmen in Clark[e] Co. Va. I have been before the civil authorities with the freedmen and they have laid their cases before them and the authorities have promised to bring the guilty parties to justice at the next Court.

I find a disposition on the part of the authorities in Clark[e] Co. Va. to postpone or put off freedmen while they can before them with complaints.

No case has been reported to me when justice was not done—when the case was tried the testimony of the freedmen is taken in all cases.[141]

Support for Education and Medical Care

One of the Freedmen's Bureau's most important tasks was supporting the education of African Americans in the Civil War's aftermath. This series of excerpts offers some insight into the level of support the Freedmen's Bureau in the Shenandoah Valley offered Freedmen's Schools. Additionally, these excerpts deepen understanding of the Freedmen's Bureau's efforts in making certain

---

[140] Letter of Captain E.H. Ripley to James Boyd Esq., May 11, 1866, Roll 89, Letters Sent, May 1866-December 1868, BRF&AL.
[141] Report of Captain E.H. Ripley, April 30, 1868, in ibid.

that the medical needs of the area's African Americans were addressed.[142]

Office Asst. Supt. Counties Rockingham & Shenandoah
Woodstock, Virginia
May 11, 1867

There has been one appropriation for furniture for this school. They are now using the colored church building, the school is quite large and increasing in size daily.

Head Qrs. 9th Sub. Dist. Va
Winchester, Virginia, May 14, 1867

The school at Harrisonburg is now held in a church belonging to the colored people, which has been repaired and furnished by the Bureau and can be used as a long as required.[143]

Report of Lieutenant J.H. Hall Requesting Medical Aid for Freedmen and Refugees in Shenandoah County, Virginia
Woodstock, Virginia, May 16, 1867

Visited the families of freedmen in all part of the county—for a year past. As the number of sick is very large, and will be still larger during the warm months I respectfully recommend that a contract be made... to give medicine and advice to Refugees and Freedmen in the County.[144]

Bureau R.F. & A.L.
Office of Counties of Shenandoah & Rockingham
Woodstock, Virginia, June 1, 1867

Drs. Irwin and Triplett[145] being the only Union Doctor[s] in this

---

[142] For additional discussions of the role of the Freedmen's Bureau in medical care after the conflict see Jim Downs, *Sick From Freedom: African-American Illness and Suffering During the Civil War and Reconstruction* (Oxford: Oxford University Press, 2012), 65-94.

[143] Statements on Freedmen's School in Woodstock and Harrisonburg, May 1867, Roll 183, Endorsements Sent, November 1865-June 1866, BRF&AL.

[144] Report of Lieutenant J.H. Hall Requesting Medical Aid, May 16, 1867, in ibid.

[145] Dr. Leonidas Triplett, born in 1811, resided in Mt. Jackson, Virginia. See 1870 Census, Mount Jackson, Shenandoah, Virginia, Roll M593-1678, Page 650A. A survey of census data did not reveal any physicians with the surname Irwin.

county, all the colored people and loyal refugees, seek advice from [him] as other doctors refuse to furnish medicine gratis. The impression also prevails amongst the freemen that Dr. Irwin has a contract to attend to them, and they come to him from all parts of this and adjoining county.

These gentlemen have never refused a single applicant to my knowledge, but the demand is so constant and heavy on account of the no. of cases caused by the bad weather that they cannot afford to supply them.

Dr. Irwin had a contract to attend the troops stationed here last spring, and can take the oath prescribed... and Dr. Triplett has served in Northern Hospitals.[146]

Report of Opening a New Freedmen's School in Front Royal, Virginia
June 29, 1867

The freedmen have opened a school in Front Royal Virginia with B.H. Roberts (col[ore]d) as teacher. They are exerting every measure to support the school once with a small appropriation of (15) fifteen dollars. [With support] from the Bureau they will be able to keep the school open the entire year.

The freedmen are working... their actions are endorsed by all like-minded men. I am confident the freedmen will be in a condition to support and take care of themselves when they are regarded [sp?] as citizens.[147]

Report of Captain E.H. Ripley to Jno. McDonnell
February 1, 1868

I have the honor to report the school for freedmen at Bentonville... under John Crawford a white man... will open Feb. 1st 1868.[148]

Captain E.H. Ripley Report on Schools to Gen. Orlando Brown
February 28, 1868

I have the honor to submit the following report of schools. The

---

[146] Statement about Dr. Irwin and Dr. Triplett, June 1, 1867, Roll 183, Endorsements Sent, November 1865-June 1866, BRF&AL.

[147] Captain E.H. Ripley on reestablishment of school in Front Royal, Virginia. June 29, 1867. Roll 89, Letters Sent, May 1866-December 1868, BRF&AL.

[148] Report of Captain E.H. Ripley to Jno. McDonnell, February 1, 1868, in ibid.

*freedmen have opened a school in Berryville the county seat [of Clarke]...
the freedmen have necessary arrangements and support to pay the
teacher, Mr. H.E. Keyes (col'd.). The school year opened the 1ˢᵗ of February
with a good number of pupils... The school in Front Royal the county seat
of Warren has been in progress longer than any other school in this
division and is operated by Mr. D.II. Roberts (col'd.)... The Bureau has
leased a building of A.J. Beecher for a school room. The freedmen are
determined to keep the school open the entire year.*

*The school at Bentonville Warren Co. is [located] in a thinly
[populated] portion of this Co. and has but few pupils, but more is expected
after the winter breaks up. The Bureau has leased a room of Geo. Payne
(col'd.) for the school. Mr. John Greenfield (white) is doing all a man can
do to open a Sunday school.*

*The freedmen in Luray County Seat of Page [are planning to
build] a house for divine worship & a school. When the house is complete
they will open a grand school & I think support themselves.*

*I have been trying to get a teacher for the Massanutten District,
Page Co.[149]*

Report of Captain E.H. Ripley
April 30, 1868

*During the past two months I have visited the schools in this 2ⁿᵈ
Division and find the schools reduced in number by the larger scholars
learning and going into the fields to work. The teachers are devoting all
their time to the small children and they are progressing with their
learning, the same interest kept up to learn to read and write by the
children.*

*It is impossible to judge of the progress of the different schools for
the largest and most learned scholars have left [the] schools.*

*I have three schools in the 2ⁿᵈ Division one (1) is kept by John
Crawford a white man. The other two (2) are kept by colored men. All the
teachers have limited education but are competent to teach freedmen in
their present state. They are doing all they can to keep up the interest of
religious meetings.*

*The schools in this Division are not disliked. No objections are
made to keep up the schools but no support will be given. No school*

---

[149] Report of Captain E.H. Ripley on Schools, February 28, 1868, Roll 89, Letters Sent, May 1866-December 1868, BRF&AL.

teachers will be counted on and in the society of white inhabitants. They will be protected by the law, but no encouragement given. In my last report I reported the school at Berryville would not be able to teach longer than May for want of support—and pupils on my last visit I was informed that the freedmen had made arrangements to pay the teacher and would keep the school open all summer.

With the support of the Bureau as far as paying the School House rent, the freedmen will be able to support the three (3) schools the entire year.[150]

Perspective from Monthly Reports

On January 29, 1866, Colonel Orlando Brown, assistant commissioner for Virginia issued Circular Order 6, which ordered Freedmen's Bureau officials to file monthly reports about the "condition" of the Freedmen's Bureau in each locality as well as highlight "the state of feeling between Whites and the Freedmen, and other facts connected with the welfare of the Freedmen."[151] The following monthly reports filed by Captain Eleazur H. Ripley, who managed the Freedmen's Bureau's operations in the counties of Warren, Page, and eventually Clarke, offers significant insight into life and race relations after the Civil War in this portion of the Shenandoah.

At the outset of the conflict Ripley enlisted in the 3rd Connecticut Infantry. After the regiment mustered out of service he served in the 8th Connecticut Infantry and rose from private to captain. At the battle of Antietam, Ripley lost his left arm. In the summer of 1863 he entered the Veteran Reserve Corps, specifically the 19th regiment. In 1866 Edward Harland, who commanded the 8th Connecticut at Antietam, observed that Ripley "was always well instructed in his duties, and zealous to perform them. He discharged the duties of every position that he held, from private to captain, to the satisfaction of his superior officers."[152]

---

[150] Report of Captain E.H. Ripley, April 30, 1868, Roll 89, Letters Sent, May 1866-December 1868, BRF&AL.

[151] Kerr-Ritchie, *Freedpeople*, 35.

[152] See letter of Brigadier General Edward Harland to Secretary of War, September 20, 1866, RG 94, Letters Received, Compiled 1863-1870, National Archives and Records Administration, Washington, D.C.

Nothing of interest has transpired during this month. Claims for work for the year all here generally [have] been settled. I have not been applied to for ass[istance] nor do I know of a single instance where either White or freedman here applied to the civil authorities to settle any claims during this month. There seems to be a good feeling existing between the whites and freedmen... the freedmen here make contracts by the month for a limited number of months for so much money. The freedmen cloth[es] himself. No vagrants all are willing to work and lead an honored life. Freedman school progressing favorably large attendance both day & night school.[153]

Freedmen's Bureau officials in Warren County seemed optimistic at the end of January 1867 that the relations between the county's white residents and African Americans would remain "good," however, one month after the above report was filed, Captain E.H. Ripley saw fractures in the relationship between both races.

Monthly Report of Captain E.H. Ripley
February 20, 1867

I find the feeling of distress increasing between the whites and freedmen much of concern... it is the expectation of the whites to get the entire control of the freedmen and the laws of the Commonwealth.[154]

Monthly Report of Captain E.H. Ripley
March 28, 1867

I have the honor to submit the following report... no complaints have been filed at this office of injustice or non- compliance by either white or freedmen during the last month. The compassion to the freedmen has

---

[153] Report of Captain E.H. Ripley January 27, 1867, Roll 89, Letters Sent, May 1866-December 1868, BRF&AL.
[154] Report of Captain E.H. Ripley, Feburary 27, 1867, in ibid.

increased very much since my last report which is accounted for in my estimation by the laws passed by Congress. Rev. M. Nickerson has closed his school at this place and gone to Harpers Ferry W. Va... the freedmen are willing to [do] all they can to support the school if a teacher [comes?] that they have confidence in. The freedmen are very anxious to keep their young children in school during the summer months.[155]

Monthly Report of Captain E.H. Ripley
May 31, 1867

During this month I have visited various sections of these two counties [Warren and Page] to investigate the condition of the freedmen in the remote districts. I have found them working faithfully & giving general satisfaction. They express themselves well satisfied with their prospects before them... the demand which exceeds the supply of labor which gives the freedmen steady employment and present payment... The freedmen are carrying all to support and elevate themselves independently of the whites. There is a growing aspiration to engage themselves into society.[156]

Monthly Report of Captain E.H. Ripley
July 30, 1867

During this month the freedmen have been busily employed & rec'd. good wages & work... No complaints have been made of the freedmen leaving their contracts when offered more wages by others. The freedmen are disposed to abide by their contract in all cases.

The freedmen are employing every opportunity to instruct themselves as to their duties as citizens. There are no freedmen in this 2nd division who are confirmed drunkers [sic], but the habit of tippling or drinking a social glass with them is common.

The freedmen here organized an association to be called the Union Relief Association which is to meet once a week for the purpose of hearing from the sick and then make provisions for their comfort as far as they can. This association is to take steps to prevent intemperance and break up this habit of drinking and lounging around and other habits that were

---

[155] Report of Captain E.H. Ripley, March 27, 1867, Roll 89, Letters Sent, May 1866-December 1868, BRF&AL.
[156] Report of Captain E.H. Ripley, May 31, 1867, in ibid.

prevalent when they were slaves. This association is formed in Warren and Page Counties and is approved & supported by the intelligent whites. They are also receiving contributions to build a church.

The freedmen are doing well in their pursuit to support a school here, and with a little help from the Bureau they will be able to keep it open the entire year.[157]

Monthly Report of Captain E.H. Ripley
August 30, 1867

During the month ending Aug 31st 1867 the freedmen have been industrious & stellar, they have not violated any contract, no complaints have been made to this office... The feeling of distrust heretofore existing between whites & freedmen has disappeared.

The civil authorities are disposed to do justice to the freedmen and there is no disposition to deprive them of justice or a hearing. The school has been closed for this month on account of extreme heat & sickness of the teacher. It will be open next month.[158]

Monthly Report of Captain E.H. Ripley
August 30, 1867

During this month two (2) freedmen have been arrested and tried by the civil authority for disturbing a religious meeting in the freedmen's church. Their names are Washington Chaman and Joseph Manseau. They were complained of by the freedmen... they were found guilty. The magistrates put them under a bond of (100) one hundred dollars.[159]

Monthly Report of Captain E.H. Ripley
September 30, 1867

The freedman in this sub. dist. remain the same as last month. The demand exceeds the supply of labor which gives them steady employment.

The freedmen in Warren & Page have [been] making preparations for the coming winter. Some have bought lots and are contemplating building themselves a home during the coming winter and spring.

---

[157] Report of Captain E.H. Ripley, July 30, 1867, Roll 89, Letters Sent, May 1866-December 1868, BRF&AL.
[158] Report of Captain E.H. Ripley, August 30, 1867, in ibid.
[159] Ibid.

The freedmen have opened their school again in this place [Front Royal] and are trying to raise money by singing weekly & keep it up during the winter. A small amount from the Bureau would [provide] them a good school during this winter.[160]

Monthly Report of Captain E.H. Ripley
November 30, 1867

During this past month the County of Clark[e] has been assigned to the 2nd division. On a tour of inspection I find a great deal of intemperance among the freedmen. They rendezvous at the county seat (Berryville) on Senseny [Road] and amuse themselves by playing ball and drinking. I requested the civil authorities to close up every place where intoxicating drink was sold. I countenanced the freedmen against disturbing the peace on Sunday. I saw some of the most intelligent and urged them a Sunday school to be opened immediately as soon as I can procure a teacher.

The freedmen have no school in Page Co. They have purchased land and intend to build a school house this winter in Luray.

Some few of the whites have told the freedmen if they did not vote with them <u>against</u> a new constitution they would turn them off or would not employ them anymore.[161] *I believe the above threats will have no weight with the freedmen. It's only intended to reduce the wages for the coming year.*[162]

Monthly Report of Captain E.H. Ripley
January 31, 1868

During this month the freedmen have been making contracts for the coming year and at about the same pay as they received last year. They are all ambitious to get homes for their families so their children can

---

[160] Report of Captain E.H. Ripley, September 30, 1867, Roll 89, in ibid.

[161] In October 1867 delegates were elected to the Virginia constitutional convention. The convention, which included twenty-five African Americans, began meeting in December 1867. Among the items the convention considered, which certainly did not sit well with former Confederates in Ripley's area of control were denying the right to vote to any former U.S. or state official who fought for the Confederacy and pushing for universal suffrage for African Americans. For additional discussion on the convention see Virginius Dabney, *Virginia: The New Dominion* (Garden City, NY: Doubleday & Co., 1956), 367-373.

[162] Report of Captain E.H. Ripley, November 30, 1867, Roll 89, Letters Sent, May 1866-December 1868, BRF&AL.

tend school... The freedmen are working faithfully to open and support schools... The school in Front Royal is still open and.... a school will open in Berryville Feby 1st 1868.

The subject of temperance has agitated in this division with some success with a small Sunday School and competent teacher it will improve reasonably the feeling the has existed here by the whites not to employ any freedmen who hold to the Republican Party.[163]

Monthly Report of Captain E.H. Ripley
March 30, 1868

During the past month I have visited the towns of this division and find the freedmen doing very well and all well satisfied with their contracts for the present year. No complaints have been made at this office by the freedmen.

The schools in this division have been kept open during this month and supported by the freedmen... During the summer months there will be a large attendance of small children at the schools in this Division. The freedmen are conducting themselves in a manner that commands the respect of all.[164]

Monthly Report of Captain E.H. Ripley
April 30, 1868

During this time I have visited the different count[ies] and towns in this Division and find the freedmen generally well treated and they are well satisfied with their prospects of pay.

No complaint has been made to me of abuse or fraud except in Clark[e] Co. where the feeling of hatred is stronger than in any other county in this Division. I have examined every case that has been forwarded or reported to me and have reported the same to civil authorities and with their assistance will have the guilty parties brought before the courts at the next term.

---

[163] Report of Captain E.H. Ripley, January 31, 1868, Roll 89, Letters Sent, May 1866-December 1868, BRF&AL.
[164] Report of Captain E.H. Ripley, March 30, 1868, in ibid.

The schools are still open and kept up by the same teachers as last month except at Berryville—Mr. Keyes has been relieved [and] Mrs. Sarah J. Jackson col'd. who is a very good teacher and will help [set] up a good school. I have advocated the temperance question and recommend the teacher to open temperance meetings and get the freedmen to join a temperance society.

The political excitement is getting quite in this Division and trouble may be anticipated during the coming months. The freedmen are still determined to adhere to the Republican Party and the employers are exerting every power in their hands to compel them to vote with them against the new Constitution.[165]

Monthly Report of Captain E.H. Ripley
May 30, 1868

During the past month nothing of interest has transpired to call the attention of the military authorities. It has been remarkably quiet. The freedmen have been busy getting their corn and other crops in the ground.

The freedmen are giving the entire attention to farming. They are leasing land or planting for a certain share of the coming crop. There is no difficulty existing between the races at this time, but there is a large amount of talk and some threats against the freedmen if they still adhere to the Republican Party & the whites say if the freedmen vote [for] the new constitution they will be driven from their work and be deprived of their homes and support in this community.

The schools are very poorly attended during this month. All that could work have been taken out and put to work to earn a living to raise a crop. There will be no school in this Division that will be properly attended until after the harvest.

The temperance question has been kept before the freedmen... the freedmen fully understand their obligations toward their families and find they cannot support them and drink at the same time. With the present wages the freedmen are and continue to be self-supporting.[166]

---

[165] Report of Captain E.H. Ripley, April 30, 1868, Roll 89, Letters Sent, May 1866-December 1868, BRF&AL.
[166] Report of Captain E.H. Ripley, May 30, 1868, in ibid.

A Sacrifice for His Country:

The Military Career and Artifacts of Captain Patrick Gallagher
84th Pennsylvania Volunteer Infantry

Roderick Gainer

Heartbroken, Anna Marie Gallagher sat down in her home in Hollidaysburg, Pennsylvania, and began to compose a missive.

Hollidaysburg Oct. 20, 1862

> *To his Excellency, President Lincoln, Father of this great Republic. This comes greeting.*
>
> *Kindly asking you to peruse my little missive and grant that, as a father has compassion for his children: through your kind instrumentality, my poor orphan children, and self may soon hear glad tidings of great joy.*
>
> *Over one year ago my husband entered the service of the United States as a Captain in the 84th Regiment of P.V. he was in the service but seven months, when at the battle of Winchester, his life fell a sacrifice for his county-When after having eaten for long years the bitter fruits of orphanage himself, it is now offered as the only sustenance for his dear children. As our Heavenly Father has told us that he would be a jealous father over the orphan—even so am I always fearing for my poor children...*
>
> *Therefore as all our hopes in this world have been given to our country, & for my children sake am now prompted to apply to you. Papers have been forwarded on to the different departments at Washington City in regard to my husband's back pay, and also a pension months ago, But [sic] my hopes are still deferred until my heart is sick. I cannot think the Government is lacking, it must be the*

Officials who have it in power, for regiment after regiment of living men have been paid off and the claims of the dead soldier still remain unsettled; and for poor orphans to live through the coming winter without a father to provide for them.

I repeat to you again, that my poor babes, alone have been induced me to communicate with you, or annoy, But [sic] knowing and feeling that you are a great and a good man, and have control over all: and that I write not in vain I await in hope, trusting you will kindly do this for one who sorrows, our prayers shall ascend for you always...

> Yours with very great Respect
> Anna M. Gallagher[167]

It is unknown if Lincoln actually read this letter. It is located in Captain Patrick Gallagher's pension file, indicating that at least someone in the Federal government moved to alleviate Anna Gallagher's plight. The little missive is but one of a few remnants of a soldier's life, one who gave everything for his country.

Born in 1828, Patrick Gallagher had a rough childhood. Orphaned at an early age, the young man of Irish decent struggled mightily to make ends meet throughout his youth. He remained close to his sister, Rosanna and managed to cobble together a sparse existence as a "laborer." Through scrimping and saving, he elevated his lot, and found his true profession in the numerous foundries that dotted the landscape around Hollidaysburg, in Blair County, Pennsylvania.

In 1852, he married Anna Moorehouse, the daughter of a prominent local businessman in a formal Catholic ceremony at St. Mary's Church of Hollidaysburg.[168] Working up his career path, he soon became a furnace manager. During this time, Gallagher became a Free Mason—no doubt aided by his becoming a Presbyterian—and began to hobnob with the town's upper crust. One of his closest friends was Postmaster William Murray, a Mexican War veteran, and presidential appointee. Unlike

---

[167] Patrick Gallagher Pension File, National Archives, Washington DC.
[168] Ibid.

Gallagher, Murray remained a practicing Catholic. Nonetheless, the two men became fast friends.

By 1860, the Gallaghers had two small children, Mary and George. In 1861, as war clouds loomed on the American horizon, Mary became pregnant with a third child. Despite his nation's initial call for volunteers, Gallagher resisted war's clarion call. He had three—soon four—mouths to feed, and few expected the conflict to last long. The disaster at First Manassas soon dispelled Gallagher's notions. The war would indeed drag on and continue to escalate. At thirty-four, Gallagher enlisted in the Army as a sergeant in August of 1861. He soon received an officer's commission and the permission to raise a company of men. He completed this task admirably, and on September 5, he had completed raising a company of local men for federal service. In November, the captain and his company joined several others at the famed training grounds of Camp Curtin, near Harrisburg, Pennsylvania.

Captain Patrick Gallagher (Roderick Gainer private collection)

The newly minted captain soon received additional good news. His friend William Gray Murray had rejoined the army. Murray, like Gallagher, had heretofore remained a passive spectator to the war's conflagration. His wife was slowly dying of tuberculosis, and Murray elected to remain with her. With her passing, Murray immediately offered his services to Governor Andrew Curtin. He received an immediate commission as colonel of volunteers on December 23, 1861. He took command and began to organize nine companies into what would soon become the 84th Pennsylvania Volunteer Infantry.[169]

Training for the 84th proceeded slowly, if imperfectly. Initially brigaded with what would become the 110th Pennsylvania Volunteer Infantry, friction soon erupted between the two regiments. About one half of the men of the 110th hailed from Philadelphia, and the city boys often ran into conflict with their rural cousins in both regiments. Fights and rioting became an almost common occurrence.[170]

The regiment's feud with the 110th soon came to an end on New Year's Eve of 1861. The 84th received orders to march to Hancock, Maryland, in an attempt to thwart Confederate general Thomas J. "Stonewall" Jackson's designs on the town and vital Baltimore and Ohio Railroad. After a brutal forced march, the regiment saw its first action at Bath on January 4 and during the retreat to Hancock the following day. While attempting to escape Jackson's clutches, the regiment forded the freezing Potomac River. Captain Gallagher, exhausted, began to sink in the river. He was rescued by the regiment's major.[171]

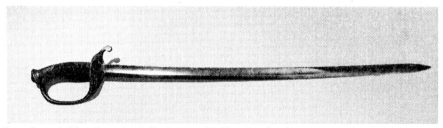

Sword carried by Captain Gallagher at the First Battle of Kernstown (Roderick Gainer private collection)

After a series of maneuvers, the regiment took part in the advance and occupation of Winchester. Attached to General James Shields's division of the Fifth Corps, the 84th served in Colonel Nathan Kimball's brigade. On March 23, 1862, they received their first real battle experience. Jackson, with a small army of under

---

[169] Roderick Rodgers Gainer, Jr. *Ultimate Sacrifice at the Battle of Kernstown: William Gray Murray, First Pennsylvania Colonel to Die in the American Civil War* (Shippensburg, PA: White Mane Books, 2007), 24-25.

[170] Ibid.

[171] *Clearfield Republican*, February 12, 1862.

4,000 men, advanced to attack what he thought was a small rear guard, only to discover—too late—that he confronted Shields's entire division of almost 9,000 men.

The 84th soon received orders to attack several Confederate batteries that plagued Kimball's brigade. The regiment moved out smartly, only to move into a murderous crossfire. While attempting to advance upon a Confederate regiment positioned behind a stone wall, the regiment halted in confusion. Patrick Gallagher—along with the regiment's other officers, attempted to get the 84th moving again. Waving his sword, Gallagher shouted "There they are boys; give it to them!" Seconds later, a bullet found his head, killing him instantly. Murray, his commanding officer and good friend, soon fell as well, in much the same manner.[172]

Gallagher's remains were returned at state expense to Hollidaysburg, where he received a lavish funeral, on the same day as Colonel Murray's. Anna Gallagher faced ruin. Not only had her husband not been paid up to that point, she had two small children and was pregnant with a third. Worse, bureaucratic woes had delayed her pension application. Desperate, she penned a letter to Lincoln (see opening of essay). Eventually, she received her pension, which brought some relief. She never remarried.[173]

Buttons from Captain Gallagher's coat (Roderick Gainer private collection)

She did retain some artifacts of her husband, however. Her efforts guaranteed that the serving military items of her husband would not lose their identity. In this she was successful. These

---

[172] *Hollidaysburg Democratic Standard*, April 9, 1862.
[173] Ibid., April 2, 1862; Patrick Gallagher Pension File, National Archives, Washington DC.

artifacts have been passed down the generations and remain with the family—my own.

The artifacts include Gallagher's Model 1850 Foot Officer's Sword, which he carried in his last battle. The sword is American made, but is otherwise unmarked. The sword is in good condition, and retains almost all of its engraving. The leather part of its scabbard has disappeared, but the mounts have been retained. Five of Gallagher's uniform buttons have also been preserved. They are all that remain of the uniform coat that disintegrated sometime in the early 20th century.

Anna and Patrick Gallagher are long deceased. Their tragedy was but one of many in the terrible American Civil War. Nonetheless, the artifacts bear mute witness, and in a sense, still speak to the terrible human cost of the war."

The Story of Two Bullets

Historic Treasures from the Virginia Museum of the Civil War and New Market Battlefield State Historical Park

Troy D. Marshall

Located in Virginia's historic and beautiful Shenandoah Valley, the Virginia Museum of the Civil War and New Market Battlefield State Historical Park tell the story of the Civil War in Virginia and one of the last major southern victories in the "Breadbasket of the Confederacy"—the Battle of New Market.

Established in 1967 by the philanthropy of Mr. George R. Collins, V.M.I. Class of 1911, the New Market Battlefield State Historical Park became a National Historic Landmark, comprising nearly 300 acres of the core battleground, the historic Bushong Farm and Hall of Valor Civil War Museum. In 2010, the museum changed its name to Virginia Museum of the Civil War to reflect its singularity as Virginia's only state-owned Civil War museum.

The building itself was designed as a monument to all valor in the battle but particularly that of the VMI cadets, the youngest combatant only fifteen years old. The brown metal rotunda is reflective of a drum with stacked bayoneted rifles. Inside the museum is an expansive red carpet symbolizing sacrifice and a gentle sweeping ramp indicative of the motion of the cadet's charge up Bushong's Hill. The Virginia Museum of the Civil War was among the top 100 structures identified as Virginia's Favorite Architecture in 2013.

Among the artifacts displayed in the museum that offers visitors a compelling story about the cadets from the Virginia Military Institute who fought at the Battle of New Market are two bullets—one representative of a close call and the other a reminder of the tragedy of armed conflict.

The first bullet, transformed into a fob, was one of two bullets that struck Cadet Francis L. Smith, a private in Company A during the Battle of New Market. Smith, a native of Alexandria, Virginia, entered the Virginia Military Institute in 1862. According to cadet biographer, Colonel William Couper, Smith "was shot in the chin, the ball entering his mouth, shattering his jawbone and coming out of his neck, just missing the carotid artery and the jugular vein. Another shot entered his shoulder and broke his collar bone—this Minie ball was later mounted."[174] In addition to the bullet, visitors to the museum can also see the uniform Cadet Smith wore during the battle, one that bears the scars of battle. Smith was one of forty-five cadets wounded during the battle.[175]

Cadet Francis L. Smith (Virginia Military Institute)

While Smith survived his wounds, largely because of the efforts of Cadet Lucien Ricketts who evacuated Smith from the battlefield, ten of Smith's comrades paid the ultimate price at New Market.[176] Among those who died as a result of wounds received at the Battle of New Market was Cadet Thomas G. Jefferson, a private in Company B, who was severely wounded by small arms fire on the

---

[174] William Couper, ed., *The Corps Forward: The Biographical Sketches of the VMI Cadets Who in the Battle of New Market* (Buena Vista, VA: Mariner Publishing, 2005), 190.
[175] For further information about the Battle of New Market see Charles R. Knight, *Valley Thunder: The Battle of New Market and the Opening of the Shenandoah Campaign, May 1864* (New York: Savas Beatie, 2010).
[176] Couper, ed., *The Corps Forward*, 190.

Cadet Smith's uniform (left) on display at the Virginia Museum of the Civil War and the bullet that struck Smith at the Battle of New Market (right) transformed into a fob (Virginia Military Institute)

afternoon of May 15. Shot through the body, two of Jefferson's comrades tried to aid Jefferson during the battle, but as one chronicler noted Jefferson was "indifferent to his own comfort" and urged those who tried to help him: 'you can do nothing for me; go to the front.'[177] After the battle, Jefferson's friend and roommate, Moses Ezekiel, found him inside of an outbuilding on the Bushong Farm. Ezekiel carried him in a wagon to the nearby Clinedinst home and did not leave his side until he died on May 18, 1864.

   A simple chunk of lead to some, the bullet taken from Cadet Jefferson's wounded body and on display at the Virginia Museum of the Civil War in New Market, offers a tangible connection to

---

[177] Charles D. Walker, *Memorial, Virginia Military Institute: Biographical Sketches of the Graduates and Élèves of the Virginia Military Institute Who Fell during the War Between the States* (Philadelphia: J.B. Lippincott, 1875), 291.

someone a contemporary believed "quiet and gentle."[178]

Cadet Thomas G. Jefferson (left) and the bullet (right) that claimed his life at the Battle of New Market (Virginia Military Institute)

---

[178] Walker, *Memorial*, 292.

"Never... More Strong and Determined"
John Mead Gould's Civil War

Nicholas P. Picerno

Of the millions of men who fought in the American Civil War arguably no one more profoundly dedicated the rest of his life to chronicling the Union war effort than John Mead Gould. Born in Bethel, Maine, on December 15, 1839, Gould attended Gould Academy (no relation) and eventually entered into the banking profession, the same occupation as his father. When President Abraham Lincoln issued his call for 75,000 volunteers in the spring of 1861, Gould wrote: "Few of us expected it, none desired it, and all were unprepared."[179]

John Mead Gould (Nicholas P. Picerno private collection)

---

[179] John Mead Gould, *History of the First-Tenth-Twenty-ninth Maine Regiment* (Portland, ME: Stephen Berry, 1871), 17.

Answering Lincoln's call, Gould took a leave from his job at the Merchants and Traders Bank in Portland, Maine, and gave the next five years of his life (1861-1866) to service in three units: the 1st, 10th and 29th Maine Infantry regiments.

Gould enlisted at the war's outset as a private in Company G of the 1st Maine. When the 1st Maine companies were reorganized in the early fall of 1861 as the 10th Maine, Gould became sergeant major. By late March 1862 Gould received a promotion to second lieutenant.[180] It was at that rank that Gould would see his first action in Virginia's Shenandoah Valley—the First Battle of Winchester.[181]

On May 27, 1862, two days after Confederate general Thomas J. "Stonewall" Jackson's victory at the First Battle of Winchester, Gould penned: "Know ye that we have done something at last. The 10th Maine has been shot at, had its courage and discipline tried."[182] Although forced to retreat with all of Union general Nathaniel P. Banks's command, the men in the 10th Maine believed they performed well considering Banks's numerical inferiority to Jackson's army. George Whitman, a private in the regiment wrote his mother: "The rebels were pretty near us, for they came in at the farther end of the city charging double quick...Our regiment kept together the best of any regt. on the retreat although they threw shell right in our midst."[183]

While some such as Whitman looked somewhat optimistically upon the regiment's conduct in its first real engagement at Winchester, others seemed dispirited. Gould penned simply: "what is known in history as Banks's retreat; and by other names, is known in our regiment as the 'Winchester skedaddle.'"[184] Gould even quipped after the fight that some men of the regiment became so frightened by the defeat at the First Battle of Winchester that there "were also a few men who kept retreating till they reached Maine or Canada."[185] The 10th Maine, which suffered a total of seventy-four casualties at Winchester (three

---

[180] For a list of promotions while a member of the 10th Maine Infantry see William B. Jordan, ed., *The Civil War Journals of John Mead Gould, 1861-1866* (Baltimore, MD: Butternut and Blue, 1997), 542.

[181] For a full treatment of the First Battle of Winchester see Brandon H. Beck and Charles S. Grunder, *The First Battle of Winchester* (Lynchburg, VA: H.E. Howard, 1992).

[182] Jordan, ed., *Civil War Journals*, 131.

[183] George Whitman letters, author's collection.

[184] Gould, *First-Tenth-Twenty-ninth Maine*, 136.

[185] Ibid., 131.

killed, six wounded, and one officer and sixty-four men captured), also had its regimental baggage captured by Jackson's command. Among the items Gould lost was his prized button collection, one he started while serving the previous year with the 1st Maine.

After the First Battle of Winchester, the 10th Maine fought with distinction in the wheat field at Cedar Mountain and the East Woods at Antietam. In the war's aftermath Gould summed up the 10th Maine's service: "We were in but two battles where we could fire our muskets. Yet in these two we lost more men in killed and wounded than any other Maine regiment had lost up to the day we left the seat of war to return home."[186]

On May 8, 1863, the 10th Maine mustered out of service; however, a number of men in the regiment signed three year enlistments. They were incorporated into the 10th Maine Battalion and were present at Chancellorsville and Gettysburg. While at home the 10th Maine veterans maintained a keen interest in the conflict and kept abreast of the trials and tribulations of the battlefield via newspapers and correspondence with former comrades who served in the 10th Maine Battalion. As time passed many of the veterans, such as Gould, yearned to serve the Union once more. That desire only increased as the Army of Northern Virginia marched into Pennsylvania in the summer of 1863.

As Confederate general Robert E. Lee's battered Army of Northern Virginia began its retreat south on July 4, 1863, Gould recorded in his diary: "We have news of three days fighting and a skedaddle by Lee. All sorts of rumors are coming over the lines. All ridiculous enough but looking as if we were once more victorious after so long a depression."[187] Later that day Gould received a copy of an order from the State of Maine authorizing Governor Abner Coburn to raise three regiments. The forming of the 29th Maine Infantry had begun.

After service in Louisiana, the 29th Maine and John Gould returned to the Shenandoah Valley in August 1864. The 29th Maine was in overall command of a general new to Gould—Philip H. Sheridan. Initially, Gould believed "Sheridan" had "the appearance of a smart man." However, Sheridan's age concerned Gould a bit. Sheridan "is young," Gould explained, "and my opinion is that if he

---

[186] Gould, *First-Tenth-Twenty-ninth Maine*, 309.
[187] Jordan, ed., *Civil War Journals*, 284.

is not hampered by the 'Chief of Staff' that he will do as well as can be done."[188] Gould's opinion of Sheridan sharply improved after their first battle together, the Third Battle of Winchester (Opequon). "Three cheers for Sheridan I say," wrote Gould just after the battle.[189]

The 29th Maine advanced onto the battlefield at Winchester on September 19, 1864, tasked with protecting the extreme right flank of General William H. Emory's Nineteenth Corps.[190] Advancing toward a position held by troops from Georgia and Alabama, the 29th Maine entered a vast field. As they approached they initially had to contend with retreating comrades from the corps' second division commanded by fellow Maine native Brigadier General Cuvier Grover. Gould described the scene in front of him: "My heart went down to my boots when I looked out to the front. There was the advance of our Second Division coming back on the dead run... By the time the Brigade had got out into the field all that part of the 2nd Division which was visible to us was in retreat and coming back pell mell upon us... There were two thousand panic stricken men coming down on us like a whirlwind it seemed. Behind them was just such a crowd of rebels all broken and loose scampering and pelting in a shot whenever they could stop to do so. There was our Brigade standing up and massed. It was awful. I don't know how the thing could have been much worse unless the rebels had been in better shape."[191]

The 29th's veterans were prohibited from firing upon the Confederates in their front due to the fear of shooting Grover's men. After Grover's division withdrew, the 29th Maine took position behind a rail fence. There the commander of the regiment, Major William Knowlton, was mortally wounded. Gould possessed profound respect and fondness for Knowlton. "Major Knowlton of our own... always seemed like a father to me and I loved him in that way," Gould recalled. He continued in admiration: "When I heard that he was mortally wounded I felt that I had almost been severed from the regiment by it. I recollected how he grasped my hand after

---

[188] Jordan, ed., *Civil War Journals*, 388.
[189] Ibid., 407.
[190] For a full treatment of the Third Battle of Winchester see Scott C. Patchan, *The Last Battle of Winchester: Phil Sheridan, Jubal Early, and the Shenandoah Valley Campaign August 7- September 19, 1864* (El Dorado Hills, CA: Savas Beatie, 2013).
[191] Jordan, ed., *Civil War Journals*, 399-400.

Cedar Mountain and said 'God bless, John, is this you?' How I wanted to have grasped his hand again today."[192]

Several days later the 29th Maine prepared for the second battle of Sheridan's 1864 Shenandoah Campaign—Fisher's Hill.[193] On September 22, the 29th Maine, along with the entire Army of the Shenandoah, received an order to "advance and carry Fisher's Hill by storm!"[194] With other Union regiments the 29th stormed the heights and aided in routing Early's Confederates. Though oftentimes dwarfed by the Third Battle of Winchester and Cedar Creek, Fisher's Hill's significance was not lost on Gould. "The battle of Fisher's Hill was one of the most singular ones of the war" he declared later. "I was so completely exhausted and yet I never felt more strong and determined in my life. Every passion which such excitement arouses was in full blast. Love, mercy, justice and every manly emotion was subdued by the *intenser* passions of destruction and hate. A man may take a gun, aim it at a rebel, shut his eyes and shoot, without but little disturbance to his inward peace, but if he undertakes to charge, charge as we did tonight, he cannot help entering the spirit of the men he goes with."[195]

After the battle of Fisher's Hill, Gould and the 29th marched south, up the Valley. On September 29 it halted at Mount Crawford. The regiment was tasked with supporting Sheridan's cavalry, which carried out its destruction of the region's mills, crops and livestock—"The Burning." Corporal Charles Corson, a member of the regiment's company D, penned a letter to his father on October 4, 1864, describing how it supported The Burning: "We have been up to Mount Crawford to support the operations of our cavalry who were burning grain, straw hay taking livestock wheat etc. this was done so that the rebs could not subsist their army and partly to subsist our army. I tell you it looks hard to see a squad of cavalry go up to a barn full of grain with large stacks of hay and straw and set fire to it."[196] Fifteen days later Corson would be shot in the head and die at the Battle of Cedar Creek.

---

[192] Jordan, ed., *Civil War Journals*, 402-403.
[193] For a full treatment of the Battle of Fisher's Hill see Jonathan A. Noyalas, *The Battle of Fisher's Hill: Breaking the Shenandoah Valley's Gibraltar* (Charleston, SC: The History Press, 2013).
[194] Gould, *First-Tenth-Twenty-ninth Maine*, 510.
[195] Jordan, ed., *Civil War Journals*, 406.
[196] Charles Corson letter, author's collection.

Corporal Charles Corson (Nicholas P. Picerno private collection)

As reveille sounded through the Nineteenth Corps' camps slightly after 3:00 A.M. on October 19, Gould and his regiment were camped near Cedar Creek just south of Middletown. Those reluctant to awaken from their slumber would soon be roused by the sound of small arms fire as Confederate cavalry probed the Army of the Shenandoah's flanks, a precursor to Early's assault against the Union army's eastern flank.[197]

Once again, as at Third Winchester, the 29th Maine held the extreme right of the Nineteenth Corps. Despite the Herculean efforts of Emory's brigades to hold their position for nearly an hour while being pressured from the south, east, and eventually the north, Emory's corps was forced to withdraw in the face of the tidal

---

[197] Although the Army of the Shenandoah's temporary commander General Horatio Wright did not demand the army rise that early, General William Emory did. For additional discussion of this early reveille and the Nineteenth Corps' preparedness to meet Early's assault see Jonathan A. Noyalas, *The Battle of Cedar Creek: Victory from the Jaws of Defeat* (Charleston, SC: The History Press, 2009), 42-43.

wave of Early's assault. Gould recalled of the corps' withdrawal: "Across the valley were the rebels, their little crossed flags as thick as ours showing that they too had hardly a hundred men to a flag. We held them every time but the order was 'retire" and so we retired, carrying our wounded to ambulances. At length after, as I judge, we had retreated two or three miles from the breast works we made a grand stand."[198]

Although driven from their camps, Early's "rout" of the Army of the Shenandoah proved temporary as late that morning General Sheridan arrived and formulated a plan to reverse the day's fortunes. When Sheridan reached his army north of Middletown, he rode among his troops and uttered words of encouragement. With spirits buoyed and a counterattack plan in place Sheridan's troops were re-energized. "History must give General Sheridan credit for doing what only such Generals as Napoleon and his kind have been able to do," Gould observed. He continued: "The halting of a whipped and disorganized army five miles from the place of attack is a feat that has not been done by many Union generals. To turn that army about and order a forward march without the help of a single fresh troop is perfectly wonderful as I look at it. To organize an army behind a fresh line is not the hardest thing in battle but to halt a few skeletons and a huge mass of stragglers can only be done by those that are born with the wonderful gift."[199]

By the end of the day Sheridan's army did the unimaginable in snatching "victory from the jaws of defeat." For Gould and his comrades delivering another, and what ultimately proved to be the final, crushing blow against Early's battered command added an additional proud chapter to the regiment's legacy. The opening line of the chapter in Gould's regimental history "Battle of Cedar Creek" succinctly captures the battle's importance in the regiment's storied service: "We count it the glory of our regiment that we fought at Cedar Creek, and that we fought so well."[200]

The 29th Maine remained in the Shenandoah Valley until April 1865. Initially they camped near Newtown, Virginia (now Stephens City). There they constructed winter quarters just south of town as part of a massive camp dubbed Camp Russell. There the

---

[198] Jordan, ed., *Civil War Journals*, 420.
[199] Ibid., 423.
[200] Gould, *First-Tenth-Twenty-Ninth Maine*, 526.

29th Maine was tasked with guarding against another possible surprise attack. At the end of December 1864, Gould (now a major) and the 29th Maine relocated their camp, along with the rest of the army, to near Stephenson's Depot north of Winchester.

29th Maine camp near Stephenson's Depot (Nicholas P. Picerno private collection)

Although Gould's military service in the Shenandoah Valley ended in the spring of 1865 he returned to the region several times after the conflict as part of gatherings of Union veterans in the Shenandoah Valley. Understanding the importance of veterans' organizations after the conflict Gould played a significant role in establishing the 1st, 10th & 29th Maine Association. Gould's passion for history, the Civil War service of the units in which he fought, and the admiration for his comrades catapulted him to the role of historian for the 1st, 10th & 29th Maine Association.

After the conflict, a pensive Gould reflected on the conflict, his military service, and the general tragedy of war. "It is a frightful record, war is a tremendous evil," Gould observed in a statement that cuts across time, "and the man who wrote of the blessings of war to a nation has different eyes from ours, and most certainly he never campaigned in Virginia and Louisiana. There is indeed a strange fascination in dwelling upon all the sad and disgusting scenes through which we have passed, but no men know better than we, what a scourge and a curse war is. If these pages anywhere convey a different idea let it be dispelled here! We are glad that we could suffer for our country's good; we glory in our strength and in all that is creditable to a soldier, but war we hate; it shall never exist again if we can prevent it."[201]

Gould perished in 1930—the last officer of all three regiments to die.

First-Tenth-Twenty-Ninth Maine Association membership ribbon (Nicholas P. Picerno private collection)

---

[201] Gould, *First-Tenth-Twenty-ninth Maine*, 614.

Book Reviews

Reflecting on a Classic

The Lower Shenandoah Valley in the Civil War: The Impact of War Upon the Civilian Population and Upon Civil Institutions. By Edward H. Phillips. Lynchburg, VA: H.E. Howard, 1993. ISBN: 978-156-1-900428.

Review by Jonathan M. Berkey

Anyone interested in the wartime experience of civilians in the Shenandoah Valley would be wise to start with Edward H. Phillips's *The Lower Shenandoah Valley in the Civil War.* Phillips, who began teaching at the Citadel in 1946, planned to revise his 1958 Ph.D. dissertation into a larger work called *War in the Land.* This project was incomplete at his death in 1973, but twenty years later H.E. Howard published Phillips's dissertation as part of its "Virginia Civil War Battles and Leaders" series.

Phillips characterizes the lower Shenandoah Valley as a border region: the economic interests of its inhabitants led them to develop commercial ties with the North and the West, while the presence of slavery in the region contributed to a sense of solidarity with the Deep South. Residents' border identity strongly influenced their sense of loyalty as the sectional crisis heated up. Most denizens believed that secession would bring disastrous results to the lower Valley. Phillips cogently observes that it was the secession of South Carolina and other states of the Deep South—not the election of Abraham Lincoln—that initiated a political crisis in the region.

Phillips describes the loyalty of lower Shenandoah residents as existing on a continuum, from what he calls Tories (the strongest Unionists) to secessionists, with various shades of intensity in between. Unionism in the lower Valley had both a geographical dimension and a class component. Unionist feeling tended to be stronger in the North and West; most mechanics and artisans embraced Unionism while the traditional social and political elite tended to be secessionists. Confederate military action, like the dismantling of the Harpers Ferry armory and attacks on the Baltimore and Ohio Railroad, strengthened Union feeling in the region. After the summer of 1861, as it became apparent that neither government could establish dominion in the lower Valley, many (though not all) civilians became convinced that a moderate policy toward neighbors of differing political persuasions would serve them best.

As civilians in the lower Valley tried to make sense of their political allegiances, they also witnessed the deterioration of their political, social, and economic institutions. In a series of thematic chapters, Phillips traces the decline of local government, churches, commerce, banks, and transportation networks as the war continued. Many government bodies and religious congregations simply stopped meeting as the exigencies of war appeared in the region. School buildings and churches were co-opted by the military to serve as hospitals and to house troops and supplies. Phillips asserts that there were some limits to this deterioration. Despite frequent disruptions, the Baltimore & Ohio Railroad was able to function throughout the war (largely due to the power and resources of the Union army), and the area's churches suffered less than other institutions because of the devoted clergy who continued to look after their flocks.

The practice of agriculture in the lower Valley remained steadfast as local institutions disappeared. While farmers close to transportation routes faced a great deal of destruction, more isolated farms remained relatively untouched. Even if they did not suffer from direct encounters with either army, most farms struggled with labor shortages as family members left to join the army and slaves fled to Union lines. Reduced but continual agricultural production allowed many residents to survive by living in what Phillips called "a raw frontier existence." (148)

By the fall of 1864, even this frontier existence was threatened by a hardening Union military policy toward civilians. Phillips points to the arrival of Ulysses S. Grant in Virginia and Philip H. Sheridan in the Shenandoah Valley as marking the beginning of a new harder style of warfare that deliberately targeted the resources of civilians. Sheridan's tactics effectively took the Shenandoah Valley out of the conflict and convinced its residents that the Confederate cause was no longer viable. By the end of the war, all that was left to lower Valley civilians was, according to the title of the book's last chapter, "A Desolation Called Peace." (149)

Unlike many other books based on unedited dissertations, *The Lower Shenandoah Valley in the Civil War* is well written and accessible to the general reader. It does, however, have some weaknesses that perhaps Phillips was planning to address in his subsequent manuscript. Although the reader quickly realizes that the lower Valley comprises Berkeley, Jefferson, Frederick, and Clarke counties, Phillips does not clearly define the region nor does he identify what made these counties distinct from the rest of the Valley. More importantly, Phillips's analysis of the region's most significant institution—slavery—shows its age. Without citing specific evidence, Phillips suggests that slavery in the lower Valley was somehow less rigorous or exploitative than in the Deep South. He implies that the demise of slavery in the region was gentler because of this. While Phillips offers insights into why some slaves remained with their masters as the war continued—he acknowledges that the proximity of Union military power weakened the institution—much of his discussion of slaves' motivations reflects the point of view of lower Valley masters. For instance, when discussing the flight of slaves from Stonewall Jackson's surging troops in May 1862, Phillips characterized their panic as "unreasoning and stupid." (115) Besides a mention of slaves providing information to Union troops, there is little sense of slaves' agency in Phillips's account.

Despite these issues, Phillips's study remains valuable not only for its attention to the civilian experience in the lower Shenandoah Valley, but also for its emphasis on the cumulative impact that the war had on civilian institutions. Phillips's work anticipated the more recent scholarship of Mark Grimsley on the evolving Union military policy toward civilians and Stephen V. Ash's work on military occupation in the South. More than fifty years after it was written, *The Lower Shenandoah Valley in the Civil War* remains relevant to modern scholarship on the Shenandoah Valley and the Confederate home front.

Jonathan M. Berkey is professor of history at Concord University in Athens, West Virginia, and the author of various essays and chapters about the Civil War era in the Shenandoah Valley.

Winchester's Three Battles: A Civil War Driving Tour Through Virginia's Most War-Torn Town by Brandon H. Beck. Winchester, VA: Angle Valley Press, 2016. ISBN: 978-0-9711950-6-6.

Review by Kenneth Noe

As I wrote elsewhere several years ago, Winchester is the kind of place where my friends not only had a Civil War monument in their back yard, but apologized that it was only one of the small ones. The visible legacy of the war permeates the city and environs over a hundred and fifty years later, and small wonder. Before and during the war, Winchester was the key northern gateway to the Shenandoah Valley. Tucked into the Shenandoah between imposing ranges of mountains, the town's vibrating spider's web of roads as well as nearby railroads linked it to much of the state and region. That commanding geographic location made it a vital spot for both sides to control. It changed hands an estimated seventy-two times and experienced three major battles. Conceivably no other place in the war was so contested. After the war, Winchester became another kind of gateway as survivors and their families began to delineate out how the conflict would be remembered north and south.

Yet despite all that history and the plentiful markers, tracking Winchester's war is not always easy. Traffic, modern development—markers in back yards—and until recently the lack of set-aside battlefield parks interfere with historians trying to follow the paths of armies. That is why Brandon Beck's new published driving tour is so welcome. A longtime resident of Winchester and a well-respected scholar, Beck knows Winchester's Civil War history perhaps better than anyone since the legendary Confederate mapmaker Jedediah Hotchkiss. Like a knowledgeable friend in the passenger seat, his *Winchester's Three Battles* will guide visitors with significant expertise toward a better understanding of Winchester's wartime history.

Beck divided the book into five sections. Three cover each of the city's three major battles, a fourth provides a useful overview of Winchester's war, and a final section details additional sites off the main tour routes, such as Stonewall Cemetery and the Old Court House. Each battle section begins with a tight but useful campaign narrative, followed by detailed step-by-step driving directions. Several maps and ample photographs—both period and modern—further provide access to important landmarks. Some of the book's most welcome features, often missing in similar works, are Beck's added suggestions and observations, including gems such as advising drivers to be careful turning around at one tight spot, to walk but not drive to another, and not to go in the homeowners' yard at all at a third stop. Anyone who has ever tried to trace an army will welcome immediately such observations. At other points, Beck the historian adds depth, as when he corrects the text of the Stephenson's Depot monument or questions the folk history of a prominent tomb's function as a warning to the enslaved. Each battle section also includes an order of battle and estimated times to completion. Finally, a useful bibliography leads visitors to more information.

Winchester's Three Battles, in short, will be most useful to anyone seeking to deepen their understanding of the city's complicated war. I can't wait to use it myself.

Kenneth W. Noe is a native of Virginia and currently the Draughon Professor of Southern History at Auburn University. He is most recently the author of Reluctant Rebels: The Confederates Who Joined the Army After 1861 (2010).

Decision at Tom's Brook: George Custer, Thomas Rosser, and the Joy of the Fight by William J. Miller. El Dorado Hills, CA: Savas Beatie, 2016. ISBN: 978-1-61121-308-9.

Review by Kevin Pawlak

History will never separate some figures from various Civil War battles—George Pickett and Gettysburg, Philip Sheridan and Cedar Creek, George Thomas and Chickamauga, Thomas Rosser and Tom's Brook, and so on. For the first time, Thomas Rosser and the battle that came to be associated most with his Civil War career come to life in William Miller's well researched and lively work. Miller does not merely recount the events of early October 1864 in the Shenandoah Valley. Instead, *Decision at Tom's Brook* is just as much the story of the leaders involved in the fight.

The Union Army, which had been plagued by one setback after another in the Valley, found its stride in that theater of war by autumn of the Civil War's crucial final year. Victories at Third Winchester and Fisher's Hill in September buoyed Northern spirits while sinking Southern ones, and the federal cavalry, much maligned by its Confederate counterpart thus far in the war, showed a determination to whip the enemy, something it proved it could do early in the campaign.

Enter George Custer and Thomas Rosser—once acquaintances, not friends at West Point, Miller points out—as the story's two protagonists. Their lives went separate ways because of the war but came together once more during the campaign in the Shenandoah Valley in the fall of 1864. Following the early Confederate defeats there, combative Tom Rosser arrived to help right the ship.

Meanwhile, the federal army continued gaining victories in the Valley, this time by torching portions of the region to deal a crippling logistical blow to the Confederacy. The Unionists then began moving northward, down the Valley, pursued hotly by Rosser and the rest of the Confederate cavalry. The two sides came to small blows as the Northerners continued their journey north. By October 8, Philip Sheridan had enough of his horsemen's retrograde movements and ordered them to turn about and strike the enemy the next day. Tom Rosser, leading a weak and outnumbered cavalry force, could only oblige the fight.

Miller next aptly describes in fluid prose the decision of Rosser to offer battle on the banks of Tom's Brook. Here, the two protagonists connect again, Custer and Rosser each exchanging bows towards the other across the battlefield, exemplifying their joy of the fight. The federal cavalry soon gave the Confederates too much to handle; the Confederate line snapped, and the Union horsemen again showed their new-found penchant for victory.

Tom's Brook and the resulting rout, labeled the Woodstock Races, was one of the most complete victories of the war. It crowned the victories the much-improved Union cavalry was stringing together and crushed their opposing cavalrymen. But for the combative Rosser, the Battle of Tom's Brook did not conclude in October 1864.

The book's final section is especially worthwhile. It weaves together the postwar memory of the fight at Tom's Brook within the larger context of the burgeoning Lost Cause. Ironically, the more Rosser sought to wash his hands of any guilt for the drubbing the Federals laid on at Tom's Brook, the more his name became associated with one of the Confederacy's most stinging and humiliating defeats.

Miller's work is a labor of love, filled with wonderful anecdotes drawn from the vast array of resources he compiled. It is a great read for many different audiences, one that touches on battle details while also bringing a human face to the decisions and horrors of war.

Kevin Pawlak is the Director of Education at the Mosby Heritage Area Association and a Licensed Battlefield Guide at Antietam National Battlefield.

The Second Battle of Winchester: The Confederate Victory that Opened the Door to Gettysburg by Eric J. Wittenberg and Scott L. Mingus, Sr. El Dorado Hills, CA: Savas Beatie, 2016. ISBN: 978-1-61121-288-4.

Review by Eric Campbell

We took the enemy by surprise in the Valley...our coming was as a thunderbolt from a cloudless sky. Winchester was [Robert] Milroy's headquarters; here he had extensive fortifications on almost impregnable hills, and there he issued his orders of oppression, while his minions permeated the valley, seizing, confiscating...all they could lay their rife hands on. But a little longer procrastination on our part, and this prolific valley...would have been a desert. Its proud people are as true as steel to the Confederacy and they have suffered immeasurably. ...notwithstanding it boasted impregnability[we] succeeded in capturing the entire garrison, its artillery, supplies and everything else, with the exception of some 800 cavalry with Milroy at their head, who succeeded in escaping. It is a matter of regret that Milroy escaped. His acts had been so oppressive and outrageous, that if caught, he would probably have met his just fate as a felon and outlaw. In the operations by which we cleared the valley...our loss, as I learn from Gen. Ewell's congratulatory order, was less than 300 killed, wounded and missing, while we captured 5,000 Yankees, with a loss of about 1,000 killed and wounded, together with their entire equipage, artillery and every thing else that renders an army effective.[202]

So wrote Captain John Gorman, of the 2nd North Carolina, in describing the Battle of Second Winchester. This lopsided Confederate victory, which cleared the Lower Shenandoah Valley of Union troops and opened the door for Robert E. Lee's second invasion of the North has, unfortunately, largely been overshadowed by the more titanic struggle at Gettysburg that followed just two weeks later.

Proof of this is the lack of studies devoted exclusively to this battle, and the fact that it took 126 years before the first one was published in 1989. *The Second Battle of Winchester, June 2-15, 1863* by Charles S. Grunder and Brandon H. Beck, (H. E. Howard, Inc., Lynchburg, Virginia, 1989) is less than 100 pages in length and provides a basic, but adequate overview of this important struggle, along with a battlefield tour. Thirteen years later, Larry B. Maier followed with his *Gateway to Gettysburg: The Second Battle of Winchester* (Burd Street Press, Shippensburg, Pennsylvania, 2002). At over 300 pages, this more complete study revealed a growing appreciation of the battle.

In 2016, however, Eric J. Wittenberg and Scott L. Mingus, authors who are both familiar with the Shenandoah Valley and Gettysburg Campaign, provided the fullest treatment yet of this underappreciated engagement with *The Second Battle of Winchester: The Confederate Victory that Opened the Door to Gettysburg.*

---

[202] Gorman to "Friend Holden," June 22, 1863, "Our Army Correspondence," unknown newspaper, unknown date, North Carolina State Archives, Raleigh, NC. Gorman had been a journalist for the *Raleigh Register* before the war, so it is likely that this paper carried his correspondence. He was captured at Spotsylvania Court House in May 1864 and was later one of the "Immortal 600" held outside of Charleston Harbor. Gorman survived the war and returned to work in the publishing business

Over 500 pages in length, the book is heavily illustrated and contains 16 maps (the most detailed and accurate ever produced of the battle) by Hal Jespersen. More importantly is the wealth of new information and sources uncovered in their research efforts. This new material allows the authors to deliver the fullest, most detailed and accurate accounting of Second Winchester yet published.

The Second Battle of Winchester not only supplies an accurate and complete accounting of the opposing armies' movements and combat that occurred, along with placing the battle in the context of the larger Gettysburg Campaign, but the authors are also to be commended for their excellent analysis of the leadership of the various commanders' decisions, and the larger impacts of the battle on the campaign and the various individuals who fought it. While it has taken 153 years, the Battle of Second Winchester has finally received the type of treatment it has long and rightfully deserved.

Eric Campbell has worked as a ranger-historian for the National Park Service for thirty-one years, at a variety of sites, including 24 years at Gettysburg National Military Park. He has been the chief of interpretation at Cedar Creek and Belle Grove National Historical Park, which interprets all of the Civil War sites in the Shenandoah Valley, since 2009.

A Saga of the New South: Race, Law, and Public Debt in Virginia by Brent Tarter. Charlottesville: University of Virginia Press, 2016. ISBN: 978-0-813938776

Review by Warren R. Hofstra

History's boneyard is filled with painfully complex and truly arcane stories. Public debt is surely one of them. But in *A Saga of the New South*, ace scavenger Brent Tarter proves us wrong. His account of how Virginia acquired its public debt beginning in 1822 and took until the mid-twentieth century to dispose of it is a big story that ranges widely in scope, depth, and consequence. As Brent, himself, might say: It just explains a darn lot.

Tarter is as much a master of detail as he is of the *longue durée*. Even in the post-mercantilist age of the 1820s, few still doubted the state's responsibility to promote economic development and at a coeval time of nascent capitalism when states, not banks, served as the largest aggregators of investment capital (only they could tax the surplus wealth of the people), Virginia began investing in the stock of internal improvement companies of its own creation. It issued bonds to help pay for better roads, new canals, and the railroad mania of the 1840s and 1850s. By the Civil War the state was in hock for more than forty-one million dollars.

The war changed everything. Virginia lost a third of its debt to the new state of West Virginia and most of its taxable assets including property in slaves with which to pay off what remained. By the terms of the 14th Amendment, Confederate states had to repudiate their war debts, but in Virginia the prewar obligation stood. Tarter's achievement lies in making good sense for the reader not only of the fiscal legislation and court battles resolving Virginia's liability, much of it now held, controversially, by Northern and English speculators, but also of the restitution of West Virginia's one-third in suits lasting until 1918. All the while he demonstrates how the debt issue affected Virginia politics for more than a century from the Civil War to the Civil Rights movement.

The short of it is that paying off the debt arrayed a newly aligned Conservative Party in the 1870s behind the forlorn hope of honoring the debt in full with interest against a more ragtag Readjuster Party, which sought to do to the debt just what its name implied in the cause of saving the solvency of the state without burdening ordinary people and securing for them the survival of the public schools. At odds in the contest were allied farmers, working people, and African Americans, many from the western reaches of Virginia including the Shenandoah Valley, who stood to benefit from the Readjuster program of shaving the debt in the interest of social services and Conservatives, who had subsumed the old planter class of eastern Virginia and its values in a powerful new coalition of commercial and professional, pro-business interests. Public debt had clearly pitted Virginians against each other along lines of class and race in a classic American tragedy. In time the Conservatives allied with the national Democratic Party and Readjusters with the Republicans. When Democrats exploited white racism to overwhelm the black-aligned Readjusters in the 1880s and gain control of every branch and major office of government, Virginia lurched into Jim Crow and a new century defined by Democratic Party dominance, white supremacy, and working-class disenfranchisement. And all this due to the obscure issue of public debt.

So much for the knacker. Thanks Brent.

Warren R. Hofstra, the author of numerous books on Shenandoah Valley history, is the Stewart Bell Professor of History at Shenandoah University.

The Risen Phoenix: Black Politics in the Post-Civil War South by Luis-Alejandro Dinella-Borrego. Charlottesville: University of Virginia Press, 2016. ISBN: 978-0-813938745.

Review by James J. Broomall

In *The Risen Phoenix: Black Politics in the Post-Civil War South*, Luis-Alejandro Dinnella-Borrego explores the powerful role of black political leadership in the postbellum South to challenge assertions that slavery, war, and violence had shattered African American communities and political life. Employing a biographical approach, Dinnella-Borrego follows the political careers of John Mercer Langston, James Thomas Rapier, George Henry White, Robert Smalls, Josiah Thomas Walls, and John Roy Lynch. The backgrounds of these men make them ideal for study because of their varied experiences: four were born into slavery, some were formally educated while others were self-taught, two were American Civil War veterans, and all were "committed to the Republican Party and represented a rural and formerly enslaved constituency." (3)

The book is composed of seven chapters that are broken down into three parts; a thorough introduction and conclusion frame the work admirably. Dinnella-Borrego argues "that many late nineteenth-century African American leaders embraced a careful balancing act between accommodation and demands for immediate civil and political equality." (13). By so doing, *The Risen Phoenix* bridges two prominent ways of viewing black politics: Eric Foner's contention that blacks viewed themselves American citizens as opposed to Steven Hahn's depiction of proto-black nationalists. (7) During celebrations over the passage of the Fifteenth Amendment, for example, African Americans affirmed their national citizenship but also extolled the "promise of the race" asserting that "black success rested on autonomy, education, and free labor." (46)

Readers of *The Risen Phoenix* will enjoy graceful prose and compelling narrative; moreover, they will witness the craft of the historian at its finest. Dinnella-Borrego acknowledges the dense historiography of his subject while maintaining a brisk, chronological narrative. He deftly uses newspaper accounts, Congressional and court records, manuscripts and correspondence to bolster his claims and bring the reader into the tumultuous political world of the post-Civil War South. Chapters are prefaced with explanatory vignettes, and thematic headers organize the content within.

Political success is often measured in tangible results. Dinnella-Borrego's protagonists fought a difficult battle against Northern racism that "played a decisive role in limiting the scope of black congressional power" as black congressmen were excluded from "high-ranking and powerful committees." (67) Nevertheless, black politicians capably represented their constituents through flexible strategies that varied by time and circumstance. Rather than a hagiographic depiction of these men, Dinnella-Borrego realistically assesses politicians working on issues that ranged from the personal to the national including payment for wartime damages; helping local businesses; dealing with pensions; finding relief for former officeholders; launching internal improvements; searching for economic opportunities for their constituents; and addressing issues such as federal appropriations and currency. Black politicians leaned heavily on compromise to navigate the labyrinth of Congress as illustrated during the postwar debates over white amnesty, for example. Such "sophisticated maneuverings and rhetorical strategies" served black leaders well during "their later advocacy for stronger civil rights legislation." (85) By the late nineteenth century, however, "the passing of so many powerful activists and national black political leaders reverberated within the black community." (210)

The Risen Phoenix is not a declension narrative but rather a tale of resiliency. Even during the darkest days of Ku Klux Klan violence and the white South's "Redemption," black congressmen continued to perform their official duties while demanding "freedom in the realm of politics" and decrying "white intimidation and violence." (125) Dinnella-Borrego's interpretation of black political representation is convincingly argued but will also elicit debate and disagreement as any good historical study should do.

James J. Broomall is the Director of the George Tyler Moore Center for the Study of the Civil War and Assistant Professor of History at Shepherd University.

The Making of a Racist: A Southerner Reflects on Family, History, and the Slave Trade by Charles B. Dew. Charlottesville: University of Virginia Press, 2016. ISBN: 978-0-8139-3887-5.

Review by Ann Denkler

Charles Dew's *The Making of a Racist* is part autobiography, part primer on scrutinizing primary sources, especially those devoted to unearthing the history of the American slave trade. As a young man growing up in St. Petersburg, Florida, in the 1950s, Dew is indoctrinated early into Lost Cause ideology and racial segregation, and he describes, with probity, his personal and intellectual struggles to "unmake" his racism. Dew recalls both an education through didactic written sources and personal episodes involving his parents and African-American community members. When the author was fourteen, for example, a family friend gave him *Facts the Historians Leave Out: A Youth's Confederate Primer*, a book that blamed slavery on the North, and, like so many postbellum texts, insisted that most enslaved individuals were treated well. Dew recalls that his father greatly admired a blistering treatise on Eleanor Roosevelt, *Weep No More My Lady,* which, as Dew notes, "...carried on the front cover a caricature of a buck-toothed Mrs. Roosevelt crying crocodile tears."(39). Dew also mentions his beloved children's book, *Ezekiel*, and how it smacked of racial stereotypes and was infused with Black dialect; he realized that the book marked "...the beginning of a long process of my education as a southerner, particularly my acculturation into the white South's racial attitudes" (37). When a local African-American man, Bill, who owned a shoe-shine parlor attempted to approach Dew's parents' house to ostensibly apologize for an incident at the store, Dew's father was enraged: Bill had broken one of the most pervasive and stolid rules of segregation—not coming to the appropriate door. Recollections like this one must not have been easy for the author to revisit and share, but they vividly reveal the extent of racism in the South.

Should anyone believe after reading this retrospective that the South's devotion to its "War of Northern Aggression" and present-day Confederate commemoration is innocuous and merely about heritage, I would be astonished. By systematically promoting the education of the "truth" of the Civil War and the justification of the racial segregation in the South, adults in Dew's world in the middle of the twentieth century purposefully sought to perpetuate a past, present, and future of prejudice and division. They also strove to sustain the mythology that the central consequence of integration was the sexual exploitation of southern white women by African-American men. As Dew's edification continues through high school and college, he continually questioned his parents' and his society's racism, but was reluctant to challenge it. When Dew does decide to confront his father in the tumultuous years of the Civil Rights movement, the outcome is moving and telling; he reveals how fear and hatred had the potential to damage and destroy families, white and African-American alike.

Dew devotes the second half of his book to an epiphany he experienced when presented with an 1860 price circular (from a larger collection) from the Richmond slave-trading firm, Betts and Gregory. For Dew, the indescribable inhumanity of enslavement reaches an apex in these kinds of sources, since the documentation shows humans only as commodities designed to bring in profits. And these profits were astonishing: in one Richmond firm alone, sales from 1859 reached 2.7 million in today's dollars.

The Making of a Racist is an engaging book I read in nearly one sitting. Clearly Dew's experiences were emotionally painful, and his attempts to overcome the heartbreak of his youth are reflected in his reading of the primary sources on Virginia's slave trade. Readers will appreciate Dew's honesty, and his prose reaffirms why I too chose to research African-American history.

Ann Denkler is an Associate Professor of History and Director of the Public History Program at Shenandoah University.

The First Republican Army: The Army of Virginia and Radicalization of the Civil War by John H. Matsui. Charlottesville: University of Virginia Press, 2017. ISBN: 978-0-813939278.

Review by Jonathan Steplyk

John Pope's Army of Virginia does not enjoy a particularly prominent or illustrious place in Civil War history. It existed as an army for only three months, occupying northern Virginia through the summer of 1862 while the Army of the Potomac fought the Peninsula Campaign. During this time, its men controlled the Shenandoah Valley, threatened Richmond from the north, and protected Washington, D.C. Forces from the Army of Virginia suffered bitter defeats, most notably at Cedar Mountain and Second Manassas. Despite its short and unprepossessing tenure, this "hard-luck" and understudied army is the source of fresh insights in John H. Matsui's *The First Republican Army: The Army of Virginia and the Radicalization of the Civil War*. An Assistant Professor of History at Virginia Military Institute, Matsui explores the highly political nature of Civil War armies, arguing that the Army of Virginia effectively "constituted the Republican Party-in-arms." (4) From its generals to the rank and file, Pope's army favored a Republican approach to winning the war, especially in terms of the destruction of slavery and bringing the hard hand of war to the Confederate homefront.

Matsui effectively presents the Army of Virginia as a Republican foil to George McClellan's Army of the Potomac. McClellan formed his army is his own image, not only in terms of military precision and professionalism but also partisan politics. Among his senior commanders he favored West Point graduates, especially men personally loyal to him who favored a Democratic limited war approach that left slavery undisturbed and safeguarded civilian property. Conversely, the Army of Virginia became home to Republican West Pointers like John Pope and Abner Doubleday as well as Republican political generals such as Nathaniel Banks and Franz Sigel. Matsui also explores how demographics shaped the political character of the two armies. McClellan's men came overwhelmingly from the Mid-Atlantic and New England states, especially from urban Democratic strongholds. Pope's army was comparatively more diverse geographically, including men from the Old Northwest and border state Unionists along with Northeasterners. Irish-Americans in McClellan's ranks brought Democratic loyalism and hostility to abolition, whereas the Germans so prevalent in Pope's army overtly opposed slavery.

The Republicanism of Pope's men also manifested itself during their occupation duty. The Army of Virginia chaffed under the policy of having to protect the property of hostile civilians whose menfolk were fighting for the Confederacy. Pope himself altered this policy in a series of orders that removed military guards from private homes and evicted male civilians who refused the oath of allegiance. Such orders drew the ire of Confederate soldiers and civilians but met with great approval among his own men, who earned a reputation as eager plunderers. Additionally, while McClellan and his cronies favored returning escaped slaves to their masters, Pope's Republicans-in-arms readily gave refuge to thousands of African-Americans who freed themselves by fleeing to Union lines.

The First Republican Army adds to the growing body of literature emphasizing the political character of Civil War armies. In addition to the partisan identity of generals, Matsui examines how political values shaped the Army of Virginia via regimental officers and enlisted men. Many Union units, Matsui reminds us, allowed the soldiers to elect their NCOs and company officers. Assigning field officers was no less political, in that their promotions were usually the prerogative of governors and because governors often deferred to the will of the regiment.

Matsui's work offers an exciting contribution to our understanding of the citizen-soldier armies that fought the Civil War. This book is essential reading for those who would better understand the war in the East, particularly the occupation of the Shenandoah Valley and northern Virginia. Moreover, *The First Republican Army* skillfully explicates how this often overlooked fighting force became a vanguard for emancipation and hard war.

Jonathan Steplyk is an instructor of history at Texas Christian University and a former interpretive ranger at Cedar Creek and Belle Grove National Historical Park.

Engineering Victory: How Technology Won the Civil War by Thomas F. Army, Jr. Baltimore: Johns Hopkins University Press, 2016. ISBN: 978-1-4214-1937-4.

Review by James Gillispie

In *Engineering Victory* Thomas Army proposes a "corrective" to the approaches of past historians that have placed primary emphasis on the war's outcome on things like generalship and political leadership as well as economic and manpower disparities. Without totally discounting such variables, Army argues that far too little attention has been paid to engineering (topographical and mechanical) in determining ultimate victory for the North. Furthermore, Army asserts that the key reasons for the North's clear superiority in engineering ability during the Civil War were both economic and cultural. The North had the edge in engineering because, "...the labor system in the North rewarded mechanical ability, ingenuity, and imagination. The labor system in the South failed to reward these skills." (5)

The book is at its best in demonstrating the importance of topographical and mechanical engineering in modern war. In that point Army is certainly correct that as Union armies invaded a massive Confederacy, the ability to build and repair roads, bridges, and railroad lines was critical. Without the ability to open invasion routes and keep supply and communication lines open, Union victory would have been considerably more difficult and may not have happened at all. In the West, Army makes very good cases that at places like Island No. 10 and Vicksburg engineering played vital roles in ultimate Northern success.

Unfortunately, Army is less convincing that engineering was *the* key variable in the war's outcome. The case is compellingly made that the North had superior engineering resources and used them effectively, but that engineering determined the results of many significant battles is questionable. During his descriptions of the Peninsula and Chancellorsville campaigns, Army appropriately points to Union engineering feats, but the North failed in both, suggesting that perhaps generalship played a key role, as many historians have argued. Inferior engineering is blamed for Lee nearly getting captured on the retreat from Gettysburg, but he still escaped. This is not to suggest Army is mistaken about engineering's importance, just that there is often insufficient engagement with existing explanations for why the North won/South lost to demonstrate that engineering was as important as generalship, resource disparities, or political leadership.

Army's argument that the North won because the free labor culture fostered educational reform and provided mechanical experience while a benighted slave culture dominated by planters who "feared...an educated yeomanry" (5) is not so much erroneous as woefully overstated. Army depicts a rather stark educational and cultural divide where educational reform and mechanical experience were substantive and widespread north of the Mason-Dixon Line while south of it a planter elite taught its citizens that "'book learn'n' was useless" (28) and that working with one's hands was for slaves. Army provides very little data to demonstrate that Northern educational opportunities were substantive or widespread and scholars will ask if Army has perhaps overstated the extent of education reform and industrialization in the antebellum North. Similarly, scholars will question if the contrast is not overstated given that the South did produce Confederate naval innovators such as John Mercer Brooke, John Porter, and Horace L. Hunley, none of whom are discussed.

Ultimately, military historians will be disappointed that in making the case for engineering being at the center of victory/defeat, the book does not substantively engage existing theories to demonstrate that engineering was as important as generalship, political leadership, and resource disparities. Scholars will also question if Army has not overstated the educational and mechanical differences between antebellum Northerners and Southerners. Nevertheless, *Engineering Victory* deserves praise for calling attention to engineering's role in the Civil War and will no doubt serve as motivation for further study, which Army does demonstrate is warranted.

James M. Gillispie, author of Andersonvilles of the North: The Myths and Realities of Northern Treatment of Civil War Confederate Prisoners, is the Dean of Humanities and Social Sciences at Lord Fairfax Community College in Middletown, Virginia.

Determined to Stand and Fight: The Battle of Monocacy, July 9, 1864 by Ryan T. Quint. El Dorado Hills, CA: Savas Beatie, 2016. ISBN: 978-1-61121-346-1.

Review by Brandon H. Beck

This is a fine book, well-researched, written, and illustrated. It would be a perfect choice for any undergraduate course in Civil War history, particularly for any institution within field trip distance of the Monocacy battlefield. It is only seventy miles from the Shenandoah University campus, and the drive there could easily follow Confederate general Jubal Early's route north. It was no skirmish, but a pitched battle for high stakes: 7,200 men were engaged (14,000 Confederates, 5,800 Federals, with a high rate of casualties, nearly 1,300 Federals and probably about 800 Confederates. It is well worth a visit or a field trip, and Ryan Quint's book includes a guided tour.

In the summer of 1864, following Grant's bloody repulse at Cold Harbor, General Robert E. Lee decided to try to repeat the great diversionary success of 1862 in the Valley. General Jubal Early, with what remained of the Second Corps of the Army of Northern Virginia, marched west into the Valley, drove Union General David Hunter away from Lynchburg, and then turned north, down the Shenandoah Valley. Quint does not take up Early's march until Chapter 2.

His first chapter focuses on the Shenandoah Valley, and its place in Confederate strategy. The lead illustration is of the Shenandoah River and there is an excellent map, entitled "The Eastern Theater." The background narrative comes down through the First and Second Battles of Winchester. By the end of the book, students will see the stage set for another Valley Campaign and the Third Battle of Winchester.

The story of Early's march down the Valley, as if "to design threatening the line of the Potomac," is clearly told. Early, of course, crossed the Potomac, which Jackson had not. Quint shows how Lincoln, Halleck, and Grant misunderstood, or underestimated, the danger in Early's march, and how a scratch force had to be assembled in time to try to slow Early's advance. Students should be directed to the importance of Chapter 4, "Sigel Delays at Harpers Ferry: July 3–6, 1864." Thus far, Early had carried out Lee's wishes perfectly. Early's own plan was to take Harpers Ferry and come down the Potomac onto Washington itself. Neither in September 1862 nor in June 1863 had Lee approached Washington. Now, in 1864, Union general Franz Sigel, in command at Martinsburg, left that post, crossed the Potomac River at Shepherdstown, and brought his force into Harpers Ferry, with a total strength of about 6,000 men. The Federal stand, on Maryland Heights, forced Early to change the axis of his advance from southeast to northeast. Going by way of Shepherdstown and Frederick brought on the collision with Wallace at Monocacy. Victorious then, Early moved on to Fort Stevens the next day. Quint well describes the physical danger Lincoln was in as he watched the engagement. Early concluded that he would get no closer to Washington.

When Early returned to Virginia, he had good reason to feel well satisfied. He had diverted two corps from the Army of the Potomac, the Sixth and Nineteenth, from Petersburg to Washington. Early would win further battles in the Valley—Cool Spring and Second Kernstown—but the mention of Petersburg had a settling effect. Grant had by then crossed the James, as if Early had not gone to the Valley at all.

This is an excellent book. The guided tour is a welcome addition, as are the author's observations of the battlefield's state of preservation. There are extremely good appendices, by Quint and others: civilian experiences at the battle, Early's attempted ransom of Frederick, Maryland, medical care (John Wynn), the plan to raid Point Lookout (Phillip Greenwalt), McCausland at Chambersburg (Avery Lentz), and Lew Wallace's literary legacy. Students will be impressed by the many ways Civil War military history "spills over" in significant ways beyond the battlefields. *Ben Hur*, of course, is here, but so is Billy the Kid, Camden Yard, and the fire engine house at Harpers Ferry. Brief unit histories are useful, and the short biographies of leaders don't interrupt the narrative.

Civil War historians, particularly those teaching anywhere near Monocacy Battlefield, need to take note of this excellent book.

Brandon H. Beck is professor emeritus of history at Shenandoah University and founding director of the McCormick Civil War Institute. He is the author or editor of numerous volumes in Civil War era history.

Notes on Contributors

Gary L. Ecelbarger is the author of seven books and a contributing author to three other works. Half of his books are dedicated to the Shenandoah Valley Campaign of 1862 as well as over a dozen magazine articles and essays focused upon the same theater. His book-length treatments of the battles of Kernstown, Front Royal and Winchester as well as his *Blue & Gray Magazine* General's Tours of Cross Keys and Port Republic have all been widely acclaimed for thorough research and thought-provoking discoveries. A twenty-year veteran of Shenandoah Valley tours, Ecelbarger is also a charter and former board member of the Kernstown Battlefield Association and has aided in the historical interpretations of several regions of the Valley in 1862. He plans to produce a book which details the final two weeks of this famous campaign.

Roderick Gainer currently works for the US Army as the command curator of Arlington National Cemetery. He has worked with Army historical collections for over twenty years and specializes in 18th and 19th century military material culture. Gainer has conducted extensive research in the role of the Shenandoah Valley in the Civil War.

Kenneth E. Koons is the General Edwin Cox '20 Institute Professor of History at Virginia Military Institute in Lexington, Virginia, where his signature course is "The History of Everyday Life." His research and writing focus on social and economic history of the nineteenth-century Shenandoah Valley. His publications include articles on the history of wheat farming in the Valley and on slavery and its aftermath in the region. He is editor (with Warren R. Hofstra) of *After the Backcountry: Rural Life in the Great Valley of Virginia, 1800-1900*. Koons has served as a consultant to museums, government agencies, attorneys, and non-profit organizations, on issues relating to the history of agriculture and rural life. He holds a Doctor of Arts Degree in history from Carnegie Mellon University.

Troy D. Marshall is an alumnus of the College of William & Mary and a graduate of the University of Oklahoma. He has worked in museums for eighteen years and held various positions at sites including the Museum of the Confederacy, Sherwood Forest Plantation, Shirley Plantation, and Pamplin Historical Park. He currently serves as the director of the Virginia Museum of the Civil War and New Market State Battlefield in New Market, Virginia. He is an active supporter of the Virginia Association of Museums and museum advocacy around the world.

Jonathan A. Noyalas is director of Shenandoah University's McCormick Civil War Institute and founding editor of the *Journal of the Shenandoah Valley during the Civil War Era*. He is the author or editor of eleven books on Civil War era history and has contributed more than 100 articles, essays, reviews, and book chapters to a variety of scholarly and popular publications including *Civil War History, Civil War Times, Civil War Monitor,* and *America's Civil War.* He is the recipient of numerous awards for his teaching, scholarship, and service including the highest honor that can be bestowed upon a professor at a college/university in the Old Dominion—the State Council for Higher Education in Virginia's Outstanding Faculty Award.

Scott C. Patchan is a graduate of James Madison University and is the author of many articles and books including *The Forgotten Fury: The Battle of Piedmont* (1996), *Shenandoah Summer: The 1864 Valley Campaign* (2007), *Second Manassas: Longstreet's Attack and the Struggle for Chinn Ridge* (2011), *The Battle of Piedmont and Hunter's Raid on Staunton* (2011), and *The Last Battle of Winchester: Phil Sheridan, Jubal Early and the 1864 Shenandoah Valley Campaign* (2013). He has also written feature essays for *Blue and Gray Magazine* on Cool Spring, Rutherford's Farm and Second Kernstown; Third Battle of Winchester, Fisher's Hill, Cedar Creek and two volumes on Second Bull Run. He has also written extensively for *Civil War Magazine, North & South, America's Civil War* and other historical publications. He is currently editing the journal of Colonel Joseph Thoburn and continuing his work on the Valley Campaigns.

Nicholas P. Picerno is chairman of the Shenandoah Valley Battlefields Foundation. During his tenure he has chaired the committees on interpretation and education and property management. In 2006, Picerno spearheaded the effort to purchase, protect and interpret the Huntsberry property on the Third Winchester battlefield, now the largest preserved Civil War battlefield in the Shenandoah Valley. He also serves on the Board of Trustees of the Lee-Jackson Education Foundation of Charlottesville and is vice-president of the Lincoln Society of Virginia. He is a former member of the board of trustees of the Museum of the Confederacy in Richmond, Virginia. Picerno has been researching the history of the 1st-10th and 29th Maine Infantry regiments for over thirty-five years. A career police chief Picerno recently retired as chief of police at Bridgewater College in Bridgewater, Virginia, where he continues to direct the Bridgewater College Civil War Institute.